Phillip M. Chen is Professor and
Chairman of the Graduate School of
European and American Studies at
Tamkang College in Taipei, Taiwan,
Republic of China, was born in
Shanghai in 1935. He received a B.A. in
1958 from Taiwan University, in 1962 an
M.A. from Marquette University and
in 1967 a Ph.D. from the University of
Massachusetts. A former State Depart-
ment scholar-diplomat to the Republic
of China, Dr. Chen has served as a
special consultant to the Ministry of
Foreign Affairs for the Republic of
China. He has taught political science
and international political theory at
Springhill College, (Mobile, Alabama)
and the University of Massachusetts.

Law
and
Justice

The Legal System in China
2400 B.C. to 1960 A.D.

Law and Justice

The Legal System in China 2400 B.C. to 1960 A.D.

Phillip M. Chen
Tamkang College

DUNELLEN PUBLISHING COMPANY
New York/London

International Standard Book Number 0-8424-0050-8

Library of Congress Catalogue Number 77-168685

Printed in the United States of America

First Edition
1973

Martin Robertson & Company Ltd - London

To My Mother

Contents

Preface ix

1 Introduction 1

2 Chinese Legal Tradition 7

The Old Law 8
The Position of Law in Traditional Chinese
    Society 11
Traditional Concepts of the Origin of Law 13
Supernatural and Law 16

3 Law as the Secondary Mediator 25

Confucian Ideology and the Chinese Law 26
The Legalists and Law 30
Li versus Law 34
Modern Law Reform 40

4 Law in Communist China 55

The Development of Chinese Communist Law   58
Legal Theory of Communist China   65
Mao's Legal Theory   79
The Role of Law — Legal or Political   87

5 The Nature of Chinese Socialist Law   103

The Principle of Socialist Legality   106
The Interpretation of Law   110
The Character and Function of Civil Law   117
The Marriage Law   128
The Application of the Civil Law   130
The Character and Function of Criminal Law   141

6 Legal Institutions of the People's Republic 167

The Organization of the Judiciary   169
The Courts   171
The People's Procuratorates   178
The Lawyer   183

7 Conclusion   203

Law and State   203
Theory v. Practice: An Evaluation   206

Bibliography   211

Index   229

Preface

The Chinese Communist Constitution and individual statutes and decrees abound with the phrase "according to the law." But the Chinese Communist conception of the nature and function of law differs sharply from that held by Western democratic states. Law is intimately associated with the idea of the nature of the state, and is considered a tool for the maintenance of state domination.

Justice has been claimed as a major aim by the Chinese Communists. They have argued that the efforts of the West to create an independent system of law courts and to provide a fair trial are designed solely to mask the injustice of the Western systems. They have declared openly that their law and courts are instruments of state policy and by no means impartial.

To write a book on Communist China's legal system at a time when it is still, for the most part, surrounded by the bamboo curtain is, in many respects, a foolhardy effort. In preparing this book, I have been keenly aware of the persistent problem of not being able to provide the most up-to-date, systematic data (if, indeed, such were available). My approach to the study of law and politics is highly eclectic. I have interpreted whatever ideas seemed useful and whatever data were accessible and relevant. I have combined various functionalist approaches with more traditional kinds of analysis.

Professor Jerome Cohen of Harvard Law School inspired my daring attempt. I am most grateful to Professors Ferenc A. Vali, Franklin W. Houn of the University of Massachusetts, my former teachers, for their unending patience in assisting both the research and the writing. Their encouragement has been the key to the completion of this study. A note of appreciation to Professor Neil T. Romans of Providence College and Victoria Ulich who read and edited the manuscript is in order. To the entire staff of the Far Eastern Law Division, Library of Congress, I owe special thanks for their service in gathering materials which I needed. I am indebted to the University Research Committee, University of South Alabama, for providing a research grant in support of this final revision.

A special word of thanks should go to Patricia Coppinger, Managing Editor of the Dunellen Company, for her pleasant and efficient cooperation.

Phillip M. Chen

Tamkang College
December, 1972

1   Introduction

We are forced to think about Communist China because of the power struggle going on in the world
today. The People's Republic appears to the Western nations primarily as a problem of foreign policy. Yet it is impossible to develop a sound foreign policy toward Communist China on the basis of
international politics alone; we cannot estimate
what its leaders want in the world merely from our
contacts with them in the Soviet Union, Germany,
Poland, Japan, Hong Kong, and other places outside
Mainland China. To understand Chinese aims and
methods abroad, we are compelled also to concern
ourselves with Chinese aims and methods at home.
We must be in a position to evaluate the strength
and weakness of the Chinese system, and the beliefs and values on which it is founded.

Law occupies a position of crucial significance,
for a legal system expresses in a most vivid and
real way what a society stands for. It represents
both what is preached and what is practiced. It

tells what is officially and publicly considered
to be right, and what is officially and publicly
done when things go wrong. Of course, what is
officially considered and done may conflict with
what is unofficially considered and done.

From a purely political viewpoint, the study
of Chinese Communist law has become a matter of
urgent practical importance. Certainly we cannot
make a peaceful settlement with Communist China
without some understanding of her legal system —
her concepts of law and justice, traditional and
Communist, as well as her actual legal practices.
Yet Chinese Communist law is not a product of
Marxist-Maoist socialism alone, and the conflict
between socialism and free enterprise is by no
means the only issue that is posed by the present
international cold war. Chinese law is also a
product of Chinese history. It is *Chinese* law —
just as American law is not capitalist law, or
democratic law, but *American* law. Each system
is a mixture not only of socialist and capitalist
features, but also of precapitalist elements stem-
ming from many different periods of past history.
Law cannot be neatly classified in terms of soc-
ial-economic forces. A legal system is built up
slowly over the centuries, and it is in many respects remarkably impervious to social upheavals.
This is as true of Chinese law, which is built on
the foundations of the Chinese past, as it is of
American law, with its roots in English and Western European history.

There is a third aspect of Chinese law which
deserves a separate identification. Implicit in
the Chinese legal system is a new conception of
the role of law in society and of the nature of
the person who is the subject of law. The Chinese
legislator, administrator, or judge plays the part
of an educator or teacher; the individual before
the law, "fajen" or "legal man," is treated as a
child to be educated and trained and made to behave.
I have called this the "Communist li" of Chinese

2

socialist law, though it should be understood that the concept of *li* does not necessarily imply benevolence.

We might study the whole legal system of Communist China historically, in terms of the traditional features of Chinese society over the past thousand years of its development. We might view the whole legal system of Communist China philosophically, in terms of the concept and philosophy of law and of man. We might investigate the system analytically, in terms of the functions and practices of a socialist legal framework. None of the three methods — the historical, the philosophical, and the analytical — gives the complete picture in itself. Together they may suggest the main outlines of the legal system of Communist China as a whole, and its main implications not only for an understanding of the People's Republic of China, but also for an understanding of Chinese law.

In Communist China, although the economic system has changed, although the goals of society have changed, although government is much more authoritarian than in the past, many of the techniques it uses are still similar to those used in the past. For example, there is an emphasis on not going to court and on settling disputes out of court through something called — perhaps a little misleading — mediation.[1] It is a process that involves a third "prestigious" party or person coming between two disputants and putting a great deal of pressure on one or both of the parties to settle the dispute outside of the formal legal institutions. This third "mediating" party preaches the values of the society. The values are different today. They are no longer Confucian values, but Marxist-Leninist-Maoist values. But many of the legal processes are strikingly similar to the traditional ones.

One of the reasons that Chinese people do not like adjudication is that control of the dispute

leaves their hands. Moreover, the Chinese traditionally have felt that going to court for a decision means that, even if you are the aggrieved
party, you do lose face. If you are not the aggrieved, you lose face because you somehow violated
the laws of society. But if you are aggrieved,
going to court is an admission that the other
person does not have sufficient respect for you
to settle properly outside of court. It is, therefore, an admission of lost face.

Another important reason that so many private
disputes in traditional China were handled by the
gentry was their connection with the bureaucracy.
The gentry were people who, even though they often
did not actually assume government office, had
qualified for it by either purchasing academic
titles or passing the academic examinations. Their
proposals for settling disputes were enforced mainly because of the prestige they acquired from being able to intervene with the governmental official. Parties to a dispute tended to go along
with what they proposed.

Today there is an entirely different social
structure in Communist China. The gentry no longer exist. But there are new prestigious, influential persons: Communist party officials and local
members of a sort of semi-officialdom are present
at the village or street corner. These persons
constitute a new type of Chinese gentry who are
again looked to for the informal settlement of disputes. Thus, although the values are different
and the criteria for prestige are different, the
functions, the roles played by these new gentry,
and the techniques used by them are quite similar
to those of the past.

The central question in this study may be thus
summarized: Is the Chinese attitude toward a system of law more influenced by Chinese tradition
than it is by the specific outlook of the Communist
regime? As Communist China becomes more obviously
distinguishable from the Soviets, we seek an ex-

4

planation in history, and there we find a great deal of support, a great deal of reinforcement for contemporary practices. Can history be said to do more than reinforce? Can it be said to "cause" these practices? Are the Communists good at invoking traditional practices only when it suits them, using techniques that are congenial to the people, but for new purposes? These are the questions with which we are dealing. Students of Communist China now are at the point of going from general inquiries into very specific inquiries. Law is one of those fields where the problems of continuity and change are fascinating.

The "bamboo curtain" surrounding Communist China has severely handicapped any attempt to study China's legal system. The revolutionary success of Communism in China in 1949 made the world's most populous country experience significant political, social, and economic changes. What about the legal system? Is Communist China an example of "a lawless unlimited power expressing itself solely in unpredictable and patternless interventions" in the lives of its people? Has the Chinese Communist government sought to follow Marx's gospel of the ultimate withering away of the state and of the law? Has Mao Tse-tung preferred Soviet practice to Marxist preaching? If so, which Soviet model has he chosen to follow — that of Stalin or that of Stalin's heirs? To what extent has it been possible to transplant a foreign legal system into the world's oldest surviving legal tradition? Should today's Chinese legal system be viewed as a unique amalgam of Communist politics and Chinese culture? To what extent has the legal system demonstrated a capacity for change since 1949? What has been the direction of that change, and what are the prospects for the future of the Chinese legal system?

The terms "Chinese Law and Justice" and "Legal System of Communist China" will at first seem to many people to be contradictory. It is widely believed that the Chinese Communist system is run solely by terror, the only principle of order being that of hierarchical subordination backed up by the "Public Security" force. From the proposition that the Chinese Communist regime places heavy reliance on the use of force, it is often deduced that the legal system of Communist China is merely window-dressing.

These are dangerous delusions, which in the long run only widen the gap of misunderstanding. They conceal the inner resources of the Chinese social order. The Chinese Communists *do* have a working legal system, founded on definite principles of law and justice.

NOTES

1. For a comprehensive discussion see Jerome A. Cohen, "Chinese Mediation on the Eve of Modernization," *California Law Review* (August 1966), pp. 1201-1226.

2   Chinese Legal Tradition

There are several striking characteristics about
the Chinese law tradition. First, more than
twenty-one hundred years ago China had a bureaucratic state that had already begun to use law
as an instrument for keeping the social order,
for expanding the power base of the government.
Long before America was discovered, China had a
well-organized legal system. It endured until
1911 as a fairly effective and stable system.

The second characteristic is the relative in-
significance which this formal legal system had
in the life of the country. This was due in
large part to the Confucian values and heritage
which put law in a very secondary, undesirable
position. Also, because of the vastness of China
and the difficulty of communications, in practice law did not reach down below the county government. Social groups — villages, clans, families, and other units apart from the formal law
courts — really played a significant role in settling disputes. The application, in other words,
to the official legal system was very rare.

Thirdly, at least in the last hundred years (1644-1912) of dynastic rule, corruption, irregularity, and many unattractive features were prominent in the administration of justice under the formal legal system.

Fourthly, in the administration of justice in China, there is no tradition of an adversary system by which an individual can defend himself against charges made by the state. Rather, the defendant is expected to rely completely on the tender mercies of officialdom. This absence of an adversary tradition is reflected even today.

The Old Law

As the civilization of China developed in isolation in the Middle Kingdom, for some four thousand years little influenced by the "barbarians" inhabiting the rest of the world, so the law of China grew in solitude, unaffected by the legal systems of the West.

According to the ancient history of China, the Emporer Huang Ti had issued orders regulating the conduct of his subjects in 2697 B.C. The five corporal punishments are said to have been ordered by the Emperor Yao (2357-2255 B.C.). The first criminal code was prepared by Li K'uei (455-395 B.C.), Minister of the State of Wei.[1]

From the period of the Warring States (403-249 B.C.) Chinese law has been influenced on the one hand by the philosophy of the Confucian school, reinforcing a traditional regard for order in the universe, the interdependence of all parts of the universe, and the moral obligation of the individual not to disturb cosmic harmony or else to suffer the consequences,[2] and on the other hand, by the philosophy of the Legalist school emphasizing the power of the state at the expense of the subject.[3] The short-lived Tsin dynasty (221-206 B.C.) unified China into a single empire, abolished feudalism, and set the pattern which continued through successive dynasties, a pattern of detailed legal codes, uniform and impartial, applying the philosophy of the Legalists.

The long Han dynasty (206 B.C.-220 A.D.) is the earliest period from which reliable materials still survive. The Han code comprised some twenty-odd principal statutes and a greater number of ordinances and subsidiary rules. Beginning with the "Statutes in Nine Sections" compiled by Hsiao Ho, the Chancellor of the Emperor Kao Tzu, the code grew by the end of the dynasty to some 26,000 articles and in excess of 7,700,000 words together with commentaries and glosses many times exceeding the length of the code itself.

It also included the official collection of rulings which had the form of law and various collections of precedents and comparable cases of a reinforcing nature useful for argumentation, without the force of law. It is evident that the legal system of the Han was highly organized and unified. The codes of successive dynasties were based in each case on the codes of their predecessors. The most notable codes were the Code of the Sui (589-618 A.D.), the Code of the T'ang (618-907 A.D.), which is the earliest code surviving intact,[4] the Code of Ming (1368-1662 A.D.) and the Code of the Ch'ing (1644-1911), the well-known *Ta Ch'ing Lu Li*, the most comprehensive legal code before the modern law reform of the Republic.[5]

All of these codes may be considered as the old law of China, as distinguished from the modern legislation adopted by the Republic of China in the first half of the twentieth century.

The old law was a product of Chinese society and reflected that society. It was for the most part penal in nature, matters of civil law being left to custom and usage and mainly to private arbitration. It was the criminal law of an absolute sovereign designed to preserve the order of heaven, to maintain the dynasty, and to keep the balance or harmony of nature. It was concerned entirely with protection against the wrongdoer; it was not primarily concerned with the protection of the accused's rights. It was designed to protect the State from the people, not the people from the State.

The old law was primarily a prescription of punishments. Not only were criminal acts punished, but any departure from prescribed forms or rituals was also punished. For example, failure to follow the required form in executing a mortgage could be punished with fifty blows of the bamboo, with death or permanent disability a likely result. In addition, the old law punished not only those long lists of acts expressly defined in the codes, but also punished acts found to be crimes by analogy after their commission; furthermore, there is a long record of punishments given for such vague crimes as impiety and improper behavior.[7]

Under the system of old law, the offender himself was not the only one to be punished, but his relatives and associates were also held collectively responsible and punishable. For certain crimes it was prescribed that "the culprit is cut in two at the waist; his father, mother, wife, children, brothers, and sisters, all without distinction between young and old, are publicly executed."[8]

The old law was subjective rather than objective; the status of the offender with relation to his victim not only determined the amount of the punishment but often determined whether any crime was committed at all. For example, the *Ta Ch'ing Lu Li* provided that:

> All slaves who are guilty of designedly striking their masters shall, without making any distinction between principals and accessories, be beheaded. If a principal or first wife is guilty of striking her husband, she shall be liable to the punishment of 100 blows; and the husband, if desirous thereof, may obtain a divorce

10

by making application for the same to the magistrate of the district. Any person who is guilty of striking of his father, mother, paternal grandfather or grandmother; and any wife who is guilty of striking her husband's father, mother, paternal grandfather or grandmother, shall suffer death by being beheaded.9

Although striking could be sentenced with death penalty in the above cases, it was, on the other hand, no crime for the master to strike the slave, the husband to strike the wife, or the father to strike the son.

As to the ferocity of punishment of the old law, however, it must not be forgotten that the need for reform of the old law does not mean that China is devoid of a legal history and equitable principles.

The Position of Law in Traditional Chinese Society

The written law of pre-modern China was overwhemingly penal in emphasis. It was primarily a legal codification of the ethical norms long dominant in Chinese traditional society. The Chinese society, traditionally, was not legally oriented, but it still produced a large and intellectually impressive body of codified law.

The emphasis on penal code in Chinese law meant that matters of a civil nature were either ignored entirely or were given only limited treatment under criminal law (e.g., property rights, inheritance, marriage). The law played only a secondary role in defending the individual rights — especially the economic rights, and not at all in defending such rights against the government or the state. The only purpose of the law was to

11

prevent and to deter the commission of criminal acts. [10]

For these reasons, the official law always operated in a vertical direction, from the state down upon the individual, rather than on a horizontal direction, between individuals.[11] No private legal profession existed to help individuals plead their cases, and even in the government itself, because law was only the last corrective measure, officials exclusively concerned with the law operated only on the higher administrative levels. On the lower level, that of the *hsien* or county, which was the level where governmental law impinged most directly upon the people, its administration of law was solely conducted by the hsien magistrate as one of several executive functions. He alone was authorized and obliged, without formal legal training, to act as detective, prosecutor, judge, and jury.[12] However, to avoid injustice on this lower level trial, a very carefully defined system of appeals existed which automatically took all but minor cases to higher levels for final judgment. Cases of capital crimes were often tried by the emperor himself.[13]

How law in traditional Chinese society became the embodiment of the ethical norms of Confucianism will be discussed later. Here it should be stressed that in China, perhaps even more than in most other civilizations, the ordinary man's awareness and acceptance of ethical norms was shaped far more by the pervasive influence of custom than by any formally enacted system of law. The clan into which he was born, the guild of which he might become a member, the group of gentry elders holding informal sway in his rural community — all of these extra-legal bodies helped to smooth the inevitable frictions in the traditional Chinese society by inculcating moral precepts upon their members, mediating disputes, or, if necessary, even imposing disciplinary sanctions and penalties.

12

The unofficial non-legal institutions were supplemented by complementary procedures on the part of the government itself which, despite their official inspiration, functioned in almost total separation from the formal legal system. These extra-legal bodies, of a police nature,[14] were what the Chinese people normally looked to for guidance, mediation, and sanction, rather than to the formal legal system per se. In the mind of Chinese people, involvement in law was generally regarded as a road to disaster and, therefore, to be avoided at all cost.[15]

Traditional Concepts of the Origin of Law

Before discussing the traditional concepts of the Chinese toward the origin of law, classification of terms is necessary. The most important word in the Chinese legal vocabulary is *fa*.[16] Fa is the usual generic term for positive or written law as an abstraction ("law" or "the law"), but it may also be used in the plural to mean separate "laws". The word was already in common use before its appearance in legal contexts. Its root meaning is that of a model, pattern, or standard; hence, of a method or procedure to be followed. From this root meaning comes the notion, fundamental in Chinese legal thinking, that fa is a model or standard imposed from above, to which the people must conform.

Another important word, perhaps even more common than fa in early legal references, is *hsing*, signifying "punishment". After the written law came into existence, however, the meaning of hsing was extended to include not only the punisment per se, but also the written prohibitions whose violation would result in these punishments. In this important secondary usage, therefore, hsing may be fairly understood in the sense of

13

"penal law" or "criminal law". The frequency of its occurrence in the early legal passages — both alone and as an alternative term for fa — is indication of the antiquity of the Chinese view which sees written law, fa, as primarily signifying penal law, hsing.

A third term, *lu*, though very important in the law codes of imperial times (221 B.C. onward), appears only rarely in a legal sense in earlier texts. As used in these codes, it is the technical designation for the major articles into which the codes are divided, and as such may be translated as "statute" or "code". *Fa-lu* means, in the modern usage, "law".

With these definitions behind us, let us now see how the ancient Chinese viewed the origins of law. It has been traditional for the Chinese to explain human events in terms of the rational, or what seems to be the rational, rather than in terms of the supernatural. In other words, a notable feature of Chinese historical and philosophical thinking, apparent already in early times, is its strongly secular tone. The legal thinking, therefore, is also entirely secular. It was suggested that law was traditionally viewed in China as primarily an instrument for redressing violation of the social order caused by individual acts of moral or ritual impropriety or criminal violence. It was further stated that such violation of human morality, in Chinese eyes, really amounted to violation of the total cosmic order.[17]

An excellent example of this attitude is a story providing probably the earliest explanation for the origin of fa, written law. The remarkable feature of this story is that it attributes the invention of fa neither to a Chinese sage-king nor even to a Chinese at all, but rather to a "barbarian" people, the Miao, alleged to have flourished during the reign of the sage Shun (23rd Century B.C.). Thus the key sentence tells us: "the Miao people made no use of spiritual cultivation, but

14

controlled by means of punishment (hsing), creating
the five oppressive punishments, which they called
law (fa)."[18] Then the text goes on to say that
many innocent people were executed by the Miao, who
were the first to administer such punishments as
castration, amputation of the nose or legs, etc.
Shang Ti or the "King on Heaven" (the supreme god
of the ancient Chinese), seeing the resulting disorder among the people, felt pity for the innocent
and hence exterminated the Miao, so that they had
no descendants.[19]

The origin of law expressed in this story no
doubt reflects a period in legal development (Sixth
Century B.C.) when written law was still a novelty
and hence was viewed with suspicion. In later
centuries, when law became more prevalent and the
need for its existence became increasingly recognized, the sociological explanations of its origin
appeared. Though their attitude toward law is no
longer hostile, they all agree with the unknown
author of the Miao legend in explaining the origin
of law in purely secular terms.

During the Han empire, the Legalist School explained that law (fa) has its origin in social
righteousness (*yi*). According to the *Huai-nan
hung-lieh chieh*:

> Social righteousness has its origin in what
> is fitting for the many. What is fitting
> for the many is what accords with the minds
> of men. Herein is the essence of good gov-
> ernment...law is not something sent down by
> Heaven, nor is it something engendered by
> Earth. It springs from the midst of men
> themselves, and by being brought back (to
> man) it corrects itself.[20]

Another important explanation can be found in
the *Treatise on Punishments and Law* of Han Shu:

> The sages, being enlightened and wise by nature,
> inevitably penetrated the mind of Heaven and

and Earth. They shaped the rules of proper behavior (li), created teachings, established laws (fa), and instituted punishments (hsing), always acting in accordance with the feelings of the people and patterning and modeling themselves on Heaven and Earth.[21]

The Supernatural and Law

A significant feature of the early written law of several major civilizations of antiquity was its close association with religion. Not all of these civilizations actually produced systems of written law. When they did so, however, they commonly expressed this content by attributing, at least initially, a divine origin to the law they used — the belief that such law had been given or revealed to mankind by a god or gods.[22]

We find Plato, in the famous opening passage of the *Laws*, making his attribute the origin of law "to a god".[23] We also find Cicero, despite the early secularization of law in Rome, similarly purporting to assert that "Law is not the product of human thought, nor is it any enactment of peoples, but something which rules the whole universe ...Law is the primal and ultimate mind of God."[24] Even in eighteenth century England, after centuries of experience with secularly-oriented common law, we find a similar conception in legal theory. Sir William Blackstone, author of the famous *Commentaries* (1765), regarded "divine law as the cornerstone of the whole (legal) edifice," and "sought to make secular law approximate to the dictates of God and of nature."[25]

Turning from Europe to Asia, we find this belief underlies Judaic and Islamic law, for those peoples needing no further elaboration. The well-known laws of Hammurabi (1728-1686 B.C.), for example, show that he received from Shamash, god of justice, a divine commission for his writing of

16

the laws.[26] In India, there is no real equivalent of the Western idea of law. The nearest approach was the concept of *dharma*, a word translatable as "law", but more properly signifying "religious law", and hence ipso facto having a connotation of divine origin.

In the history of mankind, everywhere there was a stage at which the rule of law was not distinguished from the rule of religion, and in China this stage had already been passed. On the surface, it may be difficult to trace any connection between law and religion. There is no evidence for a god-made law in China in historical time, such as the law of Hammurabi, Manu, or Moses. Nor did the ancient Chinese believe, as did the Greeks, that law was given to men by gods. The enforcement of Chinese law did not depend to any noteworthy degree upon the power of religion. No known Chinese law included a curse within its sanctions.[27] There was not a single legal authority who claimed supernatural power.[28]

Many people believed that the gods rewarded the honest and innocent and punished the evil and guilty. Sin and crime were not differentiated. At the same time, they believed that the gods knew who was good and who was bad. When men could not decide whether a person was guilty or innocent, the decision was left to the gods. Therefore, the primitive law often appealed to the gods and employed the ordeal to arrive at a judgment.[29]

In China there is no historical evidence that ordeal was ever a part of the formal legal procedure. Robson, in commenting on ordeal in general, observes that there is scarcely a country in which ordeal has not been practiced, with the possible exception of China, where there is no hint of judgment by the gods.[30] This statement is not completely accurate, but it is close enough to the historical facts. Although the ordeal was not a part of legal procedure, it should be noted that supernatural judgment was sought in other ways.

17

The Chinese people believed, indeed many still believe today, that a man's evil-doings or crimes
might escape from secular punishment, but not the
divine judgment. To compensate for the shortcomings
of judicial administration the gods and spirits
were expected to see to it that justice was more
satisfactorily done. This can be seen from the
address made by the magistrates in the annual official *li* sacrifice[31] held in each county and village. It reads:

> All the people within the territory of my
> county who are obstinate and unfilial to
> their parents, who are disrespectful to
> their relatives, who engage in sexual of-
> fences, theft, or fraud, and defy the law,
> who confound right and wrong and oppress the
> good people, who evade labor services thus
> increasing the burden of the poor people —
> such vicious and evil persons will be re-
> ported by the spirits to the God of the
> City, thus causing their crimes to be dis-
> closed and punished by the government. In
> minor cases they will be subject to beating
> and will not be considered good citizens; in
> serious cases they will be subject to impris-
> onment, banishment, strangling, or beheading,
> and will not be able to return to their vil-
> lages alive. If their crimes are not dis-
> closed, they will receive supernatural pun-
> ishment; thus all their family members will
> suffer from epidemics, and they will have
> trouble in rearing their domestic animals,
> in farming, and in their agriculture. Those
> good and upright persons who are filial to
> their parents, who are in harmony with their
> relatives, who stand in awe of the government,
> who are obedient to the rule of li and the law,
> and who do not engage in illicit activities
> will be reported by the spirits to the God
> of the City and will be protected and blessed

secretly; thus, making their families peaceful, their farms in good order, they will be able to live together with their parents, wives, and children in their villages. We, all the officials in the prefecture, who deceive the court, who are unfair to the good people, who are greedy for money and practice fraud, and whose governing is corrupt and harmful to the people — the spirits will not be partial to us and will exact retribution in the same manner.32

From the above statement it is obvious that the law depended in some degree upon the supernatural for help and that there was a close relationship between legal and religious sanctions. All the offences are obviously violations of secular and legal but not of religious obligations. Moreover, the type of sanctions emphasized was also legal and not religious. What was asked from the supernatural was help to discover criminals; the provision of sanctions was still a matter for the government. It is obvious that only when the identity of the offender could not be determined did the government ask the spirits to perform justice. We may say that religious sanctions were merely supplementary.

NOTES

1. The first Chinese criminal code, *Fa-ching liu pien (Six Codes of Law* — law of robbery, law of theft, law of arresting, law of prisonment, law of instrument (for punishment), and law of miscellaneous).

2. It might be argued that order and disorder in the world are unrelated to the maintenance or absence of law. See Wm. Theodore de Bary, ed.,

Sources of Chinese Tradition (New York: Columbia University Press, 1960), pp. 537-538. It will be discussed more comprehensively in later pages.

3. See chapter 3.

4. Y. C. Yang, *Chung-kuo chin-dai fa-chih shih (A History of Modern Chinese Legal System)* (Taipei: Chunghua Wenwoo, 1958) p. 17.

5. The last edition of which appeared in forty volumes in 1908. It was compiled in definitive form in 1740 and consisted of 436 statutes (lu)) and approximately 1,800 sub-statutes (li), available in two partial translations: George Thomas Staunton, *Ta Tsing Leu Lee, Being the Fundamental Laws, and a Selection from the Supplementary Statutes, of the Penal Code of China* (London: T. Cadell & W. Davies, 1810), and Gui Boulais, *Manuel de code chinois*, "Variétés sinologiques series 55" (Shanghai: Commercial Press, 1924). The former translates all of the statutes, but omits the sub-statutes; the latter includes Chinese text and 372 of the 436 statutes and many of the sub-statutes.

6. Crimes by analogy was done solely by the presiding official. His personal findings and analysis were the reason and the decision.

7. I.e., disrespect to any government official, or senior relatives, or using impolite language with respectable persons.

8. Staunton, *op. cit.*, p. 431. Punishment was carried out on such extensive basis because it was traditional for a family to seek revenge for harm done to one of them.

9. *Ibid.*, p. 697.

10. Many unethical or immoral acts, such as impiety, were considered as commission of crimes.

11. If a dispute involved two individuals, individual A did not bring a suit directly against individual B. Rather he pleaded his complaint to the governmental authorities, who then decided whether or not to prosecute individual B, and under what charge.

12. The magistrate was commonly assisted in his judicial work by a legal secretary who did possess specialized knowledge of the law, and who, on behalf of the magistrate, could prepare cases for trial, suggest appropriate sentences, or write the legal reports for the higher governmental authorities. Yet he was merely a personal employee of the magistrate, who paid his salary out of his own private purse. Hence the legal secretary was not permitted to try cases himself or even to be present at the trials. See Sybille van der Sprankel, *Legal Institutions in Manchu China*, London School of Economics Monographs on Social Anthropology, 24 (London: the Athlone Press, 1962), chapter 6; and T'ung-tsu Chu, *Local Government in China Under the Ch'ing* (Cambridge, Mass.: Harvard University Press, 1962), chapter 6, "Private Secretaries".

13. Ch'u, *op. cit.*, chapter 7, "Administration of Justice".

14. The *pao-chia* system of registration and crime-reporting. For a detailed description see Hsiao Kung-chuan, *Rural China, Imperial Control in the Nineteenth Century*, (Seattle: University of Washington Press, 1960), chapter 3.

15. A Chinese proverb: "Win your law suit and lose your money." Or again: "Of ten reasons by which a magistrate may decide a case, nine are unknown to the public."

16. The various meanings of fa are discussed in Joseph Needham, *Science and Civilization in China* (4 vols; New York: Cambridge University Press, 1954-1962), Vol. 2, p. 229.

17. The basic theory of the concept "the harmony of man and nature" was that the human and natural worlds are so clearly interlinked through numerous correlations that any disturbance in the one will induce a corresponding disturbance in the other. This theory developed gradually during the last two centuries of the pre-imperial period and reached a high point during the Han dynasty, when it entered the highly eclectic Confucianism which then achieved orthodoxy. By this time law had become an accepted feature of Confucian government. Parallel to this Confucianization which meant the subordination of law to Confucian li, we may perhaps speak of an analogous "naturalization" of law, which means the subordination of law to the movements of nature.

18. In *Lu hsing (Punishment of Lu)*, a section of the important classic known as the *Shu Ching (Book of History)*. For translation of the story, see James Legge, *The Chinese Classics* (5 vols., Hong Kong: Hong Kong University Press, 1960), Vol. 3, pp. 591-593.

19. See D. Bodde, "Myths of Ancient China," in Samuel N. Kramer, ed., *Mythologies of the Ancient World* (New York: Doubleday Anchor Books, 1961), pp. 389-394.

20. An eclectic philosophical work, composed by scholars attached to the Court of Liu An, Prince of Huainan (dies 122 B.C.).

21. Chapter 23, *History of the Former Han Dynasty*, written by Pan Ku around 80 A.D. For an English translation see A.F.P. Hulsewe, *Remnants of Han Law, Vol. I, Introductory Studies and an Annotated Translation of Chapters 22 and 23 of the History of the Former Han Dynasty*, "Sinica Leidensia" (Leiden: E. J. Brill, 1955), pp. 321-322.

22

22. For an excellent study on this particular subject, see William A. Robson, *Civilization and the Growth of Law* (New York: Macmillan, 1935).

23. The Athenian in the book asks his companions: "Do you attribute the origin of your legal system to a god or a man?" To which the Cretan replies: "To a god; undoubtedly we ascribe our laws to Zeus, while in Sparta, the home of our friend here, I believe Apollo is regarded as the first law-giver." Quoted in J. Walter Jones, *The Law and Legal Theory of the Greeks* (Oxford: Clarendon Press, 1956), p. 95.

24. Cicero, *De Legibus*, II, iv; translated by Clinton Walker Keyes (Cambridge, Mass.: Harvard University Press, and London: William Heinemann, 1948 reprint), p. 381.

25. Robson, *op. cit.*, pp. 47-48.

26. "Anum (the sky god) and Enlil (the storm god) named me to promote the welfare of the people, me, Hammurabi, the devout, god-fearing prince, to cause justice to prevail in the land, to destroy the wicked and the evil, that the strong might not oppress the weak." Quoted in James B. Pritchard, ed., *Ancient Near Eastern Texts* (Princeton, N. J.: Princeton University Press, 1950), p. 164.

27. The curse was used in many societies as a sanction for enforcing the law. This was practiced by the ancient Egyptians. In China, there is not a single ancient law accompanied by a curse. However, an oath which included a curse was commonly used among the people. We find in the *Chou li* that the oath was used as a means to make the parties of a contract to fulfill their obligations. Such practice is not found in later history, but the oath was commonly used as a means to force a suspect to tell the truth and to prove his innocence. The violation of an oath was itself an

23

offence against the gods. It was believed that a violation as such would cause divine punishment. Thus, many cases were not brought to court after accused persons had made an oath before the gods of a temple.

28. In many societies the administrator of justice was usually the man who possessed supernatural power, e.g., Egypt's Pharoah.

29. Ordeal was included in the Hammurabi law. It was also practiced by the ancient Greeks, the Hebrews, and many other ancient peoples. Ordeal was also practiced in the Middle Ages in Europe.

30. Robson, *op. cit.*, p. 112.

31. The li sacrifice, according to the *Ta-Ming Hui-Tien* (Code of Ming), was offered by the local officials three times a year to the spirits who had died in an unusual manner, such as accident, in battle, by execution when innocent, in epidemics, by starvation, by suicide, etc.

32. *Ta-Ming Hui-Tien*, Vol. 94, p. 151. Here the role of supernatural power on the part of officials who administered justice should also be noted. Apparently supernatural sanction was employed to check injustice in the form of an oath. Supernatural sanction was also involved in the official admonition which was issued to the officers of the local governments. This stated: "It is easier to be cruel to the small people; it is hard to deceive Heaven." (see *Ta-Ching Hui-Tien (Code of Ching)*, Vol. 3, p. 24.) Although this was not an oath, it certainly served to warn the government officials of the supernatural retribution as the result of injustice.

3

Law as the Secondary Mediator[1]

It seems imperative to describe some political characteristics of the Chinese before analyzing the Chinese legal system.

Four of the most obvious Chinese political characteristics inherited from the past have been: (1) a government of men; (2) a politics of ethics and not of law; (3) fusion of the legislative, executive, and judicial powers, and (4) implicit emphasis on the ideological power of government.

The traditional Chinese political system was fundamentally a pattern of personal relations. A people conditioned by two millenniums of monarchical and scholastic bureaucratic rule were apt to confound institutions with men. The Chinese often see through the custom or the office to the man and the role he is playing.

This intuitively realistic attitude toward life implies a recognition of the fact that institutions are always reducible to the individuals who portray them, to be strengthened by strong-willed and powerful personalities or to be weakened by timid defensive men. Furthermore, a respect for personal authority was considered not merely a cardinal principle of Confucian ethics, but a workable criterion of good human conduct. In family, as well as in government, the Chinese were customarily ruled by persons, not by laws.

Confucian Ideology and
the Chinese Law

The main characteristics of traditional Chinese law are to be found in the concept of family and in the system of social hierarchy. Since these concepts are fundamental to Confucian ideology and to Chinese society, they are also fundamental in Chinese law as well. The significance of the Chinese family concept has been widely recognized, but the importance of social status has been commonly overlooked, both by Chinese and foreign scholars, some of whom have even denied the very existence of social classes in Chinese history. In fact, however, not only did social status determine an individual's way of life, his rights and obligations under the law; it also dominated the Confucian ideology of the social order. The significance of these differences can be explained by the fact that specific laws were established to deal with them, and the maintenance of such differences was believed essential to the maintenance of legal order.

Since the relevant ideology is essential to the understanding of an institution or to the existence of a particular law, the development of law in a society must be traced in the ideology within that society. The ideologies of the Confucianists and Legalists were responsible for the traditional Chinese law.

26

The Confucian cencept, fa (law) is not the *tao* (way) to maintain the social order but the li.[2] The ruler, Confucianists insisted, must not rely primarily upon laws and punishment, but rather exhibit himself as the model for the people to follow.[3] Law and punishment were considered only the secondary or the last means to maintain the social tranquillity.

The purpose of both the Confucianist and Legalist was the maintenance of social order. The difference between them lay mainly in the problem of what constituted an ideal social order and the manner in which an order could be attained.

The Confucianists were staunch upholders of the traditional "feudal" system of values.[4] They denied that uniformity and equality were inherent in any society. They strongly believed that differences are in the very nature of things, and that only through the harmonious operation of these natural differences could a fair social order be achieved. Any attempt to equalize what was unequal, to give all men an identical treatment, would only cause an unequal or irrational division of labor and inevitably result in the destruction of the entire social order. Hence, it was natural that they should be hostile to the new law.[5] They gradually, although reluctantly, accepted law as a necessary evil when it became increasingly apparent that law had come to stay. However, they insisted that law was not necessary in the ideal state, and government by law should always be retained as the secondary choice.[6]

In order to relate Confucian ideology to the Chinese legal system, it is necessary to discuss briefly their concept of inequality of men and different social status.

The Confucianists claimed that men were born unequal by their intelligence and virtues, and these unequal characteristics set the stage for the division of labor. This inequality was based on personal ability rather than birth or economic

27

status. There were two types of laborers: the mental and the physical. It was the function of the latter group to serve the mental-labor class with their production and their services. The scholar and governmental official belonged to the first group, and it was their function to study, acquire virtue, and govern the people. Each class had its duties and obligations. Mencius asserted that "Great men have their proper business, and little men have their proper business...Some labor with their minds, and some labor with their strength. Those who labor with their minds govern others; those who labor with their strength are governed by others. Those who are governed by others support them; those who govern others are supported by them. This is a principle universally recognized."[7]

To the Confucianist the differences in nearness and remoteness, in superiority and inferiority, and in seniority and juniority that operated within a kin group, and the differences in superiority and inferiority within society at large were of equal importance.[8] These differences were indispensable to the maintenance of the social order. In other words, the social order was the sum total of these two kinds of social differences.

Therefore, the most essential factor for an orderly society was that a man's status be clearly defined, and that his roles be properly performed.[9] This depended not upon the rule of law but upon the presence of a body of approved behavior patterns, the li.[10] The function of li was to achieve social differentiation. It was the function of li to discriminate between persons according to their different social statuses. Hence, "the path (tao) of human life cannot be directed without its distinctions; no distinction is greater than social distinction; no social distinction is greater than the rule for proper conduct."[11]

On the other hand, the Confucianists believed that the rules of li were found in certain broad

28

moral principles which give the li their validity. These principles are rooted in human nature; in other words, they represent what men in general instinctively feel to be right. It is this interpretation of li which has caused some scholars to compare Confucian li with the Western concept of natural law, the Legalist fa with Western positive law.[12]

Therefore, li are preventive in that they turn the individual away from evil before he has the chance of committing a crime, whereas law (fa) is punitive in that it only comes into action to punish wrongdoer. The li derive their universal validity from the fact that they were created by the intelligent sages of antiquity in conformity with human nature and with the cosmic order. Law has no moral validity because it is merely the ad hoc creation of modern men who wish, by means of it, to generate political power.

The Confucianists firmly believed that a government based on virtue could truly win the hearts of men; one based on force could only gain their outward submission.[13] The li are persuasive and, hence, the instrument of a virtuous government; laws are compulsive and the instrument of a tyrannical government. Laws are no better than the men who create and execute them.[14] The moral training of the ruler and his officials counts for more than the devising of a clever legal system. Hence, the rules of li do not reach down to the common people and the punishments do not reach up to the officialdom.[15]

Li was important because it put a great instrument in the hands of a ruler. The so-called governing by li is much more than the application of abstract ethical and moral principles.

Li and law are obviously different rules of behavior. The Confucian School stressed the dependence on li to maintain the social order and its implementation by moral education, while the Legalist School employed law for the same end but employed punishment as the enforcement.

The Legalists neither denied nor objected to the social status distinctions made between noble and humble, superior and inferior, elder and younger, near and remote,[16] but they considered these matters minor and irrelevent, and even a hindrance to the process of governing. The Legalists were mainly interested in maintaining legal and political order, and they stressed that the governing of a state depended primarily upon the rewards which encouraged good behavior and the punishment which discouraged bad behavior.[17] The actions to be rewarded or punished were determined by objective, absolute standards which permitted no differentiation on the basis of personal differences. Only when there was a uniform law, a uniform system of reward and punishment, could everyone be forced to obey and justice be maintained. The Legalists did not deny the reality of social differentiation, but they refused to permit this reality to exert any influence over the law. In other words, the Legalists maintained that all must be equal before the law. Kuan-tzu (7th Century B.C.) stressed that government would be successful when the ruler, the minister, the superior, the inferior, the noble, and the humble all abided by the same law.[18] Han Fei-tzu (233 B.C.) said, "The law does not favor the nobles...However the law is applied, the wise have no way of avoiding (punishment), and the brave do not dare to argue. To punish a fault does not exempt the great officials. To reward merit does not exclude the commoners."[19] Such a formulation was diametrically opposed to the tenet of the Confucianists that the high officials be exempted from legal penalties.

The Lord of Shang (338 B.C.), commenting further on this point, also said, "Merit acquired in the past should not cause a decrease in the punishment for demerit later, nor should good behavior in the past cause any derogation of the law for wrongdoing later. If loyal ministers and filial sons do wrong, they should be judged according to the full measure of their guilt, and if amongst the officials who have to maintain the law and to uphold an office, there are those who do not carry out the king's law, they are guilty of death and should not be pardoned. Their punishment even should be extended to their families for three generations (San Tsu)."[20]

A spirit such as this, which never compromised, refused to consider the private affections, and was determined entirely by objective standards, contrasts sharply with the Confucian principle of government, which advised that judgments always be based on consideration of all the different circumstances and not on the general laws on punishment.[21] The Legalists objected to deliberations of this kind. They firmly insisted that law or the legal system for a social order not be changed because of the will of the ruler. The Lord of Shang also said, "The rulers of the world frequently give up the law and trust to private deliberations. This is why the state is in disorder. The early kings hung up the scales and fixed the length, and they are still followed because their measurements are clear. If the scales are discarded for measuring weight and the rule is abolished for judging length, even if accurate, (the method) will not be employed by the merchants because of its uncertainty. Those who turn their back upon the law and depend upon private deliberations do not recognize the analogy. Only the sage was able to judge the wise, the able, the virtuous, and the unworthy without the law. But not all persons in the world are sages. Knowing that personal deliberation and private approval were not reliable,

31

the early kings formulated law and made the distinction clear."[22]

To the Confucianists, the degree of intimacy between relatives was the foundation of human relationships.[23] According to Mencius, "If each man would love his parents and show the due respect to his elders, the whole land would enjoy tranquillity."[24] But the Legalists held that "when one loves his relatives, he will show discrimination; when one loves a private (person), he will be partial. If the people are numerous and engaged in discrimination and partiality, this will lead to disorder."[25] For this particular point, we shall see in later chapters that Communist China adopted precisely the same view towards individual family and relatives.

The Legalists strongly insisted that blood members of the family could be punished, relatives could be punished, but the law could never be put aside. The Lord of Shang analyzed the disadvantages of affection towards one's relatives as follows:

> The rule by means of virtue, the people will love their relatives; (to rule) by means of evil[26] the people will love the regulations ...When (the government) displays virtue, transgressions will remain hidden; when (the government rules) by means of evil, crimes will be punished. When the transgressions remain hidden, the people are superior to the law. When the crimes are punished, the law is superior to the people. When the people are superior to the law, there will be disorder. When the law is superior to the people, the army will be strong.[27]

In summary, the Legalists' attitude towards law can be stated: (1) Since a great majority of men are motivated by self-interest, severe punishments are necessary. Law is concerned with the many who are selfish, not with the few who are good.[28] (2) Law is the key path to a stable government because it provides an exact instrument with which to measure individual conduct. A government based on li cannot lead to stability, since the li are unwritten, particularistic, and subject to arbitrary interpretation.[29] (3) A good and strong government must not allow privileges and factionalism. Hence it is imperative for it to promulgate its law to all and to apply them impartially to everyone regardless of social status and personal relationships.[30] (4) For a successful legal system, the population should be grouped into units of families, and within each unit every individual should be equally responsible for the wrongdoing of every other individual, and equally subject to punishment if he fails to inform the authorities of each wrongdoing.[31] (5) Since history changes, human institutions must change accordingly. In antiquity people were few and life was easy, but today the growth of population has resulted in a sharpening struggle for existence. This is why the traditional li are no longer suitable to the social changes and should be replaced by a system of law. Law should certainly not be changed arbitrarily; yet if it is to retain its vitality it should equally be kept responsive to the changing needs of the society.[32] (6) A strong state is the one that maintains a single standard of morality and thought for its people. All private standards or values must be suppressed if they conflict with the public standards as prescribed by law. (This is precisely what Communist China is advocating today.) (7) Laws, once sufficiently established, will no longer have to be applied, since their mere existence will be enough to punish wrongdoing. Thus, harsh laws, though painful in their immediate effects, lead in the long run to an actual reduction of governmental control and to a society of freedom and equality.[33]

It may be briefly restated that the Confucianists relied on li which distinguished between individuals according to certain recognized moral criteria for the maintenance of social order. The Legalists, on the other hand, strongly opposed such discriminatory and inegalitarian rules, and insisted on the uniformity or equality for all under the law.

Li versus Law

It would be incorrect to say that Legalism in China did not leave a lasting mark on law. Its influence probably explains, for example, the continuing penal emphasis found in all of the imperial codes, and the resulting fact that their treatment even of administrative and other noncriminal matters usually follows a standard formula: Anyone who does x is to receive punishment y. The Legalists' influence also expalins certain important features of imperial juridical procedure: the nonexistence of private lawyers; the assumption (nowhere explicitly stated but everywhere implied in the treatment of defendants) that a suspect must be guilty unless and until he is proven innocent; and the legal use of torture for obtaining confession from suspects who stubbornly refuse to admit guilt despite strong evidence against him.

Besides these influences of Legalism, the most significant phenomenon of imperial times and even after the founding of the Republic is what has been termed the Confucianization of Law — that is, the incorporation of the spirit and sometimes of the actual rules of the Confucian li into the legal codes.

Of all the differences between Legalist fa and Confucian li, none is more basic than the universalism of the former — egalitarian treatment for all under the law — as against the particularism of the latter — inegalitarian treatment according to individual social status, relationship, and specific circumstances.34

After the collapse of feudalism (221 B.C.) the empire was under the control of a highly centralized government. Under this new political structure the change in the legal system was noteworthy. First, the laws of the various feudal states were no longer in force. Law became centralized under the sovereign, not the feudal nobles. The emperor alone was above the law, and the law became his instrument. Everyone within his realm, nobles and commoners, the ruling class and the ruled, came under his jurisdiction and had to obey the same law. The nobles and officials were no longer exempted from legal punishment.

From the time of Ch'in (221-207 B.C.) and Han (206 B.C.-A.D. 220), the legal system was quite egalitarian by nature, but there were still inequalities between the nobles and officials on the one hand, and the common people on the other. Despite the Legalists' insistence on equality before the law, such an equality remained unrealized because the Confucianists, after defeating the Legalists, regained their influence in the Han government. The law still recognized privileged groups — a special privileged class which included those who qualified under the "eight conditions for considerations,"35 and certain other officials not included in the above category as well as the family members of those persons.

Unlike the common people, the nobles and officials were not under the jurisdiction of the ordinary legal system. As a rule, the authorities had no right to arrest or investigate them unless permission to do so had been granted by the emperor. It was a "law" in Han dynasty that when nobles and officials from certain ranks were guilty, special permission had to be requested from the emperor before they were arrested or even investigated.36 The Code of Ming and the Code of Ch'ing both legalized this special privilege for those who qualified under the "eight conditions for consideration". They were not subject to the ordinary law. The law-enforcing officials had first to report the case to the emperor and arrest depended upon his decision alone.[37] In the Yuan Dynasty (A.D. 1279-1368), accused officials could be tortured only when the evidence clearly indicated a guilt which they had refused to confess. Under Ming (A.D. 1368-1644) and Ch'ing (1644-1912), the law was in this respect similar to that of Tang.[38] In Ch'ing's law, the permission of the emperor had to be obtained if officials of the third rank and above were to be tortured.[39]

This special legal privilege also indicated that, after investigation, they could not be sentenced unless authorized by the emperor. In T'ang (A.D. 618-907) and Sung (A.D. 960-1279) times, only those qualified under the "eight conditions for consideration", whose crime was *not* among the ten capital crimes,[40] were considered for special privilege. The law of Ming and Ch'ing contained similar legal privileges for those who qualified under the "eight conditions for consideration" no matter whether their crimes rated banishment, imprisonment, or even the death sentence.[41] Even governmental officials who did not qualify under the "eight conditions for consideration" could not be sentenced by the judicial authorities.

It is clear that under such a legal system, the judicial authorities had neither the power of investigation in most cases nor the power of sentence for those nobles and officials who committed crime. Since the law was not definitely codified in such cases, a substantial flexibility was possible.

The law of Ming and Ch'ing permitted fewer legal privileges than the laws of earlier dynasties. Officials were subject to penal law by imprisonment and banishment, but not by corporal punishment.[42] However, disputes between commoners on the one hand and nobles and officials on the other, entailed serious inequalities.

Finally, the legal privileges of officials during litigation in court were still maintained. Government officials were ashamed of being summoned to the court, especially to stand before the court with the common people. The law, therefore, did not give equal recognition to officials and commoners. No matter whether the official was the plaintiff or the defendant, he was granted the "unequal" legal privilege to decline to appear before the court with the opposing party, if the latter was a commoner. Under no circumstances was a commoner permitted to sue an official in the court, nor was an official required to defend himself before the court. Ming and Ch'ing law held that officials involved in lawsuits concerning marriage, debt, or property, could send their family members or servants to represent them in the court.

In traditional Chinese society, class distinctions were expressed socially, politically, and legally. Class consciousness played a significant role in the operation of the inegalitarian law system.

In the preceding sections we have discussed at some length the dependence of the Confucian School on li to maintain the social order and its implementation by moral education, while the Legalist School invoked law for the same end, and insisted on punishment as the means of enforcement. Li and law are obviously different rules of behavior. Since the Confucianists strove to maintain a clearly differentiated social order and relied on differentiated modes of behavior (i.e., li) to maintain it, while the Legalists strove only to maintain the legal order of the state and relied on a uniformed rule of behavior (i.e., law) to achieve this end, no compromise was possible at this point.

The conflict between rule by morality and rule by punishment is of a different kind. Moral influence and punishment are merely different means of enforcement. The problem of the li or law is fundamental; the problem of whether to use moral influence or legal punishment for enforcement is secondary. In other words, it is possible to enforce the same norm by different sanctions. The li can certainly be enforced by moral or ethical principles, but if they are enforced by legal means they do not lose their original character, and the ideal goal of the Confucianist would still be attainable.

In fact, the Confucianists never completely rejected the legal sanction, but only objected to the substitution for a moral principle of legal punishment. They never absolutely opposed the use of legal punishment, but held that the moral principle was fundamental, and the legal method supplementary. In other words, law was considered useful, but as the "secondary mediation". Law was recognized as an instrument for the legislation of morality. In addition, they argued that as soon as the process of moral influence was completely established, the function of law would cease.

Confucianism exerted an even more direct influence on the administration of justice. As government officials, the Confucianists assumed judicial responsibility and contributed to the wide discussion of legal problems. Legislative and judicial functions were not separated from executive power in the Chinese political tradition. The local chief executives were judges, and theoretically speaking, all officials, no matter what their functions, were permitted to discuss legislative and judicial problems and make suggestions. Frequently, judgments based on Confucian theory went beyond the article of the law, for the traditional Chinese system allowed considerable freedom in interpreting and applying the law. Besides, Confucianism was still held in the highest esteem, and its ethical principles were more respected than legal authority.

After Han (206 B.C.-A.D. 220), the formulation and revision of the law fell into the hands of Confucian scholar-officials who seized the opportunity to incorporate as many as possible of the ethical principles of Confucianism (li) into the law.[43] Despite the efforts of the Legalists, however, the Confucian philosophy came to dominate all traditional Chinese law.[44] The close relationship between the li and the law is apparent in the codes of the various dynasties and even after the modern law reform.[45] Originally, the various rules of behavior were regulated in detail in the books of li. Later, when the law was codified, the behavior prescribed by li was incorporated into the law. What was approved by li was, thus, also approved by law and considered as legal. The relation between li and law was obviously close.[46]

Originally, li were enforced by social sanction, and later by legal sanction. A rule of behavior enforced by social sanction is li, and by legal sanction is law. It is obvious that the same normative behavior may be subsumed under li and law concurrently. Thus, the later Confucianists used political and legal power to enforce their rules of behavior, but these norms were still included in their books of li and they still sought to enforce them by morality and education. Li and law, though separate entities, were supplementary to each other. As the norms were simultaneously sustained by both social and legal sanctions, they established an effective legal system and imposed a strong compulsion on the members of the society.

The above discussion supports the hypothesis that the family and social status were fundamental features in Chinese traditional law. This law fully recognized the parents' authority to control their children. The latter had no independent right to own private property, to live separately from their parents, or to choose their own spouses. The law also recognized the supremacy of seniors and husbands over juniors and wives. Disputes between and persecution of family members were always judged according to an individual's status in the kin group. The principle of concealment[47] and others also indicated the dominance of family ethics in Chinese law.

The Chinese legal system recognized the different status of nobles, officials, and commoners. The laws regulated an individual's way of life in accordance with his social and legal status. Above all, individuals of different status were not treated equally under the law. Nobles and officials enjoyed certain legal privileges, whereas the common people were legally unprivileged. The emphasis on social status led to the development of inegalitarian law which was specific as to status, whether family or social. Such a body of law corresponded with the doctrine of Confucianists who considered that family and social status were the essential norms of li and the fundamentals of the social order. We can therefore, conclude that Confucianism, especially the doctrine of li, dominated both law and society in traditional China. There were no fundamental changes in law throughout the history of China as far as family law and class differences were concerned until the promulgation of modern law.

Modern Law Reform

The necessity for radical reform of the old law, which had developed in isolation for many centuries, was finally recognized in the last years of the Ch'ing Dynasty. Military defeats had demonstrated that, in certain respects, China had lost legal sovereignty. Extraterritorial rights in China had been assumed by the foreign powers on the excuse of the primitiveness of Chinese law and law courts. It was widely believed that modernization of the law would assist China in over-

coming her weakness and would eliminate the demand
for extraterritoriality. The commissions for modern law reform were established by imperial edict
to draft civil, criminal, and commercial codes.
After a comparative study of penal codes of the
Western nations, a new Ch'ing Criminal Code was
placed in effect in 1910. This code abolished the
punishments of decapitation and lingering death,
and prohibited torture to extort confession.

The Revolution of 1911 ended the Ch'ing dynasty and established the Republic. The new government made all Ch'ing laws tentatively applicable
in the Republic except those contrary to the form
of the state, or contrary to the political system
of the Republic.[48] The Provisional Criminal Code
of 1912 provided, for the first time, that no person might be found guilty of an offence other than
one expressly provided for in the code, a total
change from the dynastic codes which had permitted
crimes by analogy. This code also ended the principle of collective responsibility of the family
and clan for the crimes of members, and adopted
a more reasonable method in the legal procedure
for examining the accused. No violence, threats,
inducements, fraud, or other improper means were
to be used.

After the Northern Expedition and the establishment of the National Government in Nanking in
1928, a new Criminal Code and a new Code of Criminal Procedure were enacted. These new laws bor-
rowed a significant part of the Anglo-American law.
For example, the arrested person should have the
right to a Writ of Habeas Corpus.[49] The new Civil
Law also contained democratic and egalitarian principles. For example, women were to have equal
rights under the law.[50] They were, however, enacted hastily and did not reflect the development
of post World War I criminal legislation in the
rest of the world, nor did they contain in full
the more completely developed political and social
ideas of Dr. Sun Yat-sen and the revolution.[51]

Later, the Legislative Yuan took over the revision
and codification projects, and, after commissions
had compared the modern laws of Italy, Spain,
France, Germany, Switzerland, Russia, Poland,
Czechoslovakia, Turkey, and Japan, the modern reformed laws of China were codified and promulgated in 1935.[52]

The first decade of the National Government
was a time of great progress in many fields — in
economic development, in social and educational
transformation, in political unification, and in
the elevation of China's standing in international
relations. In spite of some shortcomings, this
was a promising period of great progress, often
forgotten today. Perhaps the most important ac-
complishment of the National Government was the
introduction of a system of modern laws, codes of
procedure, and a system of law courts which began
to function and grew in importance, and, if given
time, might well have led to the establishment of
a society based on the rule of law. The Civil Code
rather than the Criminal Code laid the foundation
of the legal system. Corporation laws, banking
laws and other commercial laws followed in later
years. They were applied by a system of newly
established courts, from the District Court up to
the Supreme Court, whose decision became the last
word in the implementation of the law.

It is true, however, that this rapidly developed legal system was at first uneven. Courts in
the rural areas were not always up to standards,
and the rules of the modern laws, as well as the
codes of procedure, were not universally accepted.
Practices based on the moral code of the past,
though no longer preserved by the educational system or the elite brought up in it, still lingered
on even in the cities. In other words, the modern
legal system, which ran counter to traditional
laws, was simply not applied. Professor Escarra,
the French jurist, who wrote one of the best known
books in Chinese law, gives examples of the law

of inheritance, and many other rules that could not be applied because of the disapproval of the Chinese society. The actions of the military, not only under the "individual law" of some of the more or less autonomous warlords, but even in the central provinces under the National Government itself provide a further limitation on the law.[53] But these limitations seemed temporary. The legal administration was growing, and in time the remnants of traditional moral beliefs might have been fused with the interpretation of modern law.

The disappearance of the old social order and the rule of its moral code made imperative the acceptance of a new legal system. Under the influence of the West, the Chinese legal system was based upon the system of Western law,[54] the law that would guarantee the realm of the freedom of the individual, and the equality for all before the law. Unfortunately, the Chinese legal system never did fulfill these ideal purposes.

All this ended with the military conquest of the Chinese mainland by the Communists.[55]

NOTES

1. "Social meditation is primary, adjudication is secondary" has deep root in both traditional and modern China.

2. The term li is usually translated rites, ceremonies, courtesy, or propriety. It has been frequently referred to as "rules of behavior" or "rules of proper conduct." But, according to Confucian thought, li is a body of special rules of behavior which vary according to one's status. Since no English equivalent could include all these features, it probably would be better to transliterate. For a detailed discussion of the

43

meaning of li, see Fung (Feng) Yu-lan, *A History of Chinese Philosophy*, translated by D. Bodde, Vol. I (Peiping, 1937; Princeton, N. J.: Princeton University Press, 1953); Vol. II (Leiden, 1953).

3. For a brief but comprehensive treatment on Confucian concept with respect to virtue and force, see Franklin W. Houn, *Chinese Political Tradition* (Washington: Public Affairs Press, 1965), pp. 109-110.

4. In feudal times, the law became the instrument for ruling the people. The nobles were not subject to the jurisdiction. It was said, "Li is not applicable to the common people, punishment is not applicable to the *ta-fu* (officials)" See James Legge, *The Texts of Confucianism* (4 Vols. Oxford: Clarendon,1885), III, p. 90. And the Pai-hu t'ung explained that the li operated for the intelligent and punishment for the non-intelligent, and that officials were exempted from punishment to honor them. See Tjan Tjoe Som, *Po Hu T'ung, The Comprehensive Discussion in the White Tiger Hall* (2 Vols. Leiden: E. J. Brill, 1952).

5. For the criticism on the promulgation of penal law by Confucius, see Legge, *The Chinese Classics* (Hong Kong: Hong Kong University Press, 1960) Vol. 5, p. 732.

6. "A government based on li functions harmoniously because the li, being unwritten, can be flexibly interpreted to meet the exigences of any particular situation. A government based on law creates contention because its people, knowing in advance what the written law is, can find means to circumvent it, and will rest their sophistical arguments on the letter rather than the spirit of the law." Legge, *Chinese Classics*, Vol. 5, pp. 609-622.

7.   From *Meng-tzu chu-su* Legge, *Chinese Clas-sics*, II, pp. 125-126. The small men, i.e., the farmers, the artisans, and the merchants.

8.   For Confucianism, a line was inevitably drawn between the superior and the inferior which led to an inegalitarian relationship in the soci-ety. "This is the pervading rule of the universe." See H. H. Dubs, *The Works of Hsuntze* (London: A. Probsthain, 1928). The distinction between noble and humble, superior and inferior were based upon the talent and virtue of each person of the soci-ety, and constituted a type of social selection conditioned by individual social success.

9.   A society in which honorableness and hum-bleness, superiority and inferiority, seniority and juniority, nearness and remoteness were clearly defined constituted the ideal society; and con-versely, a lack of distinction was extremely re-pugnant to the Confucian ideology.

10.   See supra, note 2.

11.   Dubs, *op. cit.*, pp. 71-72. Similar em-phasis on this point is also found in other sources: "Li are the rules of propriety, that furnish the means of determining the relatives, as near and remote; of settling points which may cause sus-picion or doubt; of distinguishing where there should be agreement, and where difference; and of making clear what is right and what is wrong." (*Li chi chu-su*, Legge, *Texts of Confucianism*, Vol. III, p. 63).

"Hence the rules of proper conduct (li) are to ed-ucate and nourish. When the superior man has got-ten its education and nourishment, he also esteems its distinctions. What are meant by its distinc-tions? There are the classes of the noble and the base; there are the inequalities of the senior and the younger; there is what is appropriate to those who are poor and those who are rich, to those who are unimportant and those who are important." (Dubs, *op. cit.*, p. 214.)

"Hence, the ancient kings invented the rules of proper conduct (li) and justice (yi) for men in order to divide them; causing them to have the classes of noble and base, the disparity between the aged and the young, and the distinction between the wise and the stupid, the able and the powerless; all to cause men to assume their duties and each one to get his proper position." (Ibid, p. 65.)

"The ancient kings hated any disorder, and hence, established the rules of proper conduct (li) and justice (yi) to divide the people, to cause them to have the classes of poor and rich, of noble and inferior, so that, everyone would be under someone's control." (Ibid, p. 124.)

12. Joseph Needham, *Science and Civilization in China* (New York: Cambridge University Press, 1962) Vol. 2, pp. 530-532.

13. "Lead the people by regulations, keep them in order by punishments (hsing), and they will flee from you and lose all self-respect. But lead them by virtue and keep them in order by established morality (li) and they will keep their self-respect and come to you." Confucius in *Analects*, II, p. 3.

14. "laws (fa) connot stand alone, and analogies cannot act themselves when they have the proper man, they survive; When they lack the proper man, they disappear. Law is the basis of good government, but the Superior Man (chun-tzu) is the origin of the law." Legge, *Texts of Confucianism*, p. 436.

46

15. *Li Chi* (Record of Li). The statement
here made, that the officialdom (to which the Con-
fucians themselves belonged) is not subject to the
penalties of the common people, was to assume key
importance, as we shall see, in imperial Chinese
law.

16. For instance, Han Fei-tzu, the leading
representative of the Legalist School, says, "The
noble and the humble do not trespass against each
other, and the simple and the wise each has his
place — this is the perfect order." W. K. Liao,
The Complete Works of Han Fei Tzu (London, 1959),
I, p. 46.

17. The Kuan-tzu named orders, punishments,
and rewards as three instruments for governing a
state. "If it is impossible to give a reward when
someone has merit, and impossible to punish when
someone is guilty, it will be impossible to govern
the people." *Ibid.*

18. *Kuan-tzu*, a work attributed to Kuan Chung
(7th Century B.C.). See Lewis Maverich, T'an
Po-fu, and Wen Kung-wen, *The Kuan-tzu* (Carbondale,
Ill., 1954.)

19. Liao, *op. cit.*, p. 45.

20. J. J. L. Duyvendak, The *Book of Lord
Shang, A Classic of the Chinese School of Law*
(London: The University of Chicago Press, 1928),
p. 279; cf., Hulsewe, *op. cit.*. Vol. I, 112 ff.

21. Legge, *Chinese Classics*, Vol. V, Part II,
p. 609.

22. Duyvendak, *op. cit.*, pp. 261-262.

23. In the *Li Chi*, "Thus, the course of humanity was all comprehended in the love for kindred."

47

(Legge, *Texts of Confucianism*, IV, p. 66); "Benevolence is (the chief element in) humanity, and
the greatest exercise of it is in the love of relatives." (*Ibid.*, p. 312); "Affection towards relatives was considered one of the nine standard
rules to follow for a government." (*Ibid.*, p. 314.)

24. Legge, *Chinese Classics*, II, p. 178.

25. Duyvendak, *op. cit.*, p. 225.

26. Grammatically, Duyvendak's translation is
correct. However, his terms "to employ" can hardly be understood. Why did the Legalists want to
employ "wicked officials" (by means of evil) in
the government? How could the wicked make the
people love the law? The Legalists did not believe that government had to be run by the virtuous men, but neither by wicked officials. The
function of law, as they saw it, was not to en-
courage and reward the good, but to prohibit and
punish the evils. Thus, they were primarily concerned with evil. The Chinese language referred
to the method of governing, not the employment of
officials. The philosophy can be explained as
this: If a government is concerned with virtue,
then, to love one's relatives will be considered
virtue, the people will tend to conceal their
faults. If a government is concerned with evil
(outlaws), the evil will be discovered, and people
will be encouraged to report them and to regard
law as the primary importance. (See Duyvendak,
op. cit., pp. 207; 233-288.) This leads to the
further conclusion that people should be treated
as evil and governed as evil.

27. Duyvendak, *op. cit.*, p. 207.

28. "When punishments are heavy, the people
dare not transgress, and therefore there will be
no punishments." Duyvendak, p. 288.

29. "For governing the people there is no permanent principle save that it is the laws (fa) and nothing else that determine the government. Let the laws roll with the times and there will be good government..." See Chapter 54 of the writings of *Han Fei Tzu* in W. K. Liao's translation, *op. cit.*, Vol. 2, p. 328.

30. "If the law (fa) is not uniform, it will be inauspicious for the holder of the state... Therefore, it is said that the law must be kept uniform. It is out of this that preservation or destruction, order or disorder, develop, and this it is that the sage-ruler uses as the great standard for the world...All beings and affairs, if not within the scope of the law, cannot operate... When ruler and minister, superior and inferior, noble and humble, all obey the law, this is called great good government." *Kuan-tzu*, Chapter. 45 as quoted in Fung Yu-lan, *op. cit.*, Vol. I, p. 322.

31. This system was developed later known as the Bao-chia, see *supra* note 14, Chapter 2, in the Republic of China, and the Commune system in Communist China.

32. It is a similar view that Communist China takes toward traditional Chinese code of li and the necessity of law.

33. Since severe punishments served the function of "abolishing penalties by means of penalties," the Legalists believed that although the law was cruel, there was no other way to apply it. If pain was suffered for a short time the benefits would be permanent. See Duyvenak, *op. cit.*, pp. 259, 285.

34. This particularism we find perpetuated in the imperial codes. For example, homicide is differentiated by the Ching Code in its treatment

of the subject into more than twenty varieties.
(For detailed description see Boulais, *Manuel du
code chinois*, (Shanghai: Commercial Press, 1924
Nos. 1211-1343.) In view of the universalistic
nature of Legalist law as against the Confucian
interest in particular differences, a Confucian
derivation seems much more likely. In accordance
with the rules of li, the penal codes which differ
sharply according to the relative class status of
the offender and his victim, e.g., the Ch'ing Code
treats the offence of striking or beating another
person differently. Such an act, when occurring
between equals (a commoner striking a commoner,
or a slave beating a slave), is punishable by
twenty blows of the small bamboo. (Boulais, No.
1344.) For a slave who beats a commoner, however,
this normal penalty is increased by one degree
to thirty blows, and reduced to ten blows for a
commoner who beats a slave. Decapitation is the
penalty for a slave who strikes his master, there is
no penalty for a master who injures a slave.
Boulais, Nos. 1387, 1390; cf. Chu, *Law and Society
in Traditional China* (Paris and the Hague: Mouton
& Co., 1961), pp. 191 and 193. The penalty for
beating the presiding official of one's own local
community is three years of penal servitude, whereas for beating an official of other districts the
penalty differs from two years downward depending
on the official rank. (Boulais, Nos. 1367-1368;
Ch'u, p. 183). Besides providing penalties that
individually differ according to the social status,
the codes also recognize entire categories of persons as deserving of special judicial procedure
which distinguishes them as a whole from the great
majority of commoners. These groups are: members
of the imperial family, descendants of former imperial families, members of government officialdom,
and their immediate relatives.

35. The *pa-yi* "the eight conditions for consideration", which are found in the *Chou li* were:

(1)   those who were the relatives of the sovereign;
(2)   those who were old friends of the sovereign;
(3)   those who were of great virtue; (4)   those
who were of great ability; (5)   those who were
meritorious; (6)   those who were high officials;
(7)   those who were exceptionally zealous of government duties; (8)   those who were the guests of
the sovereign (descendants of the preceding imperial families). Boulais, op. cit., pp. 32-33.

36.   For a detailed discussion on this subject
see Hulsewe, *op. cit.*, Vol. I, p. 286.

37.   *Ming lu li* (Code of Ming), Vol. I, 6a;
Ch'ing lu li (Code of Ch'ing), Vol. 4, 25a; Staun-
ton, *Ta Tsing Leu Lee* (London: T. Cadell and W.
Davies, 1810) p. 7; Boulais, *op. cit.*, p. 34.

38.   *Ming lu li*, Vol. I, 28, 19b; *Ch'ing lu li*,
Vol. 4, 36, 49a; Staunton, pp. 441-442; Boulais,
p. 716.

39.   *Ch'ing lu li*, Vol. IV, 26a; Boulais, *op.
cit.*, p. 34.

40.   *Shih-o*, "the ten sins" or the "ten capital crimes", which were excluded from the pardon
of the emperor. They were: (1) rebellion; (2)
treason against the emperor; (3) betrayal to the
enemy; (4) perverse offences against parents and
other seniors (i.e., to beat or to murder one's
grandparents or parents, to murder one's paternal
uncle or their wives, father's sisters, elder
brothers and sisters, mother's parents, husband,
or husband's grandparents or parents); (5) massacre
(i.e., to kill three or more persons in one family); (6) filial impiety; (7) disrespect to the
emperor; (8) discord in families (i.e., to murder or to sell a fourth degree relative); (9)
unrighteousness (i.e., to kill a local official
by the people, or kill one's teacher, not to wear
mourning for one's husband etc.); (10) incest.

(For a detailed discussion, see *T'ang lu su-i*, I, 44b-21a; *Sung hsing t'ung* (Criminal Code of Sung), I, 5a-b; *Ming lu li*, I, 4a-5a; *Ch'ing lu li*, 4, 18a-19b.

41. *Ming lu li*, I, 6a; *Ch'ing lu li*, IV, 25a; Staunton, *op. cit.*, p. 7; Boulais, *op. cit.*, p. 34.

42. *Ming lu li*, I, 19a-23a; *Ch'ing lu li*, IV, 7a-b, 10a-b, 60a; Staunton, pp. 10-11; Boulais, p. 42.

43. For detailed discussion see Ch'u T'ung-tsu, *Chung-kuo fa-lu chih ju-chia-hua (Confucianization of Chinese Law)* (Peking: National Peking University Press, 1948) pp. 6-14.

44. Jean Escarra, "Law, Chinese," *Encyclopedia of Social Sciences* (New York, 1933), Vol. IX, p. 251; cf. his *Le droit chinois* (Peking: Henri Vetch, 1936) tr. G. R. Browne (Harvard Law School, 1961) (Xerox reprint) pp. 13-19; 70; 435.

45. This even can be found in the laws of Communist China, i.e., Article 8, Chapter III, *The Marriage Law of the People's Republic of China*, stated: "Husband and wife are in *duty* bound to love, respect, assist and look after each other, ..." Article 13, Chapter IV of the same law, "... the children have the duty to support and to assist their parents..." The filial piety implicit in the familistic ideal was also strongly stressed by the Confucianists. According to li children should serve their parents dutifully. This respect will be discussed in later chapters.

46. The people frequently mentioned li and law together, and such terms as li fa or li lu (li and law) were common in legal writings.

47. "A father should conceal the fault of a son and that a son should conceal the fault of a

father." For a comprehensive treatment see Prof. Ch'u T'ung-tsu, *Law and Society in Traditional China*, pp. 70-74.

48. Yang, *A History of Modern Chinese Legal System* (Taipei: China Culture, 1958) pp. 49-50.

49. *Ibid.*, p. 74.

50. *Ibid.*, p. 144.

51. For the legal theory of the modern law reform in China, see *Ibid.*, pp. 124-142.

52. Yang, *op. cit.*, pp. 146-148. An excellent analysis on the legal theory of the modern Chinese law, see Roscoe Pound, "Comparative Law and History as Bases for Chinese Law." *Harvard Law Review*, Vol. 61, (May, 1948), pp. 749-762.

53. For instance, the frequent notices in Chinese newspapers in the city that proudly announced the arrest and execution of bandits or robbers without the slightest reference to any formal court procedure. This was not under martial law, but in an area and time under a normally functioning administration. It did not occur to any person to question such citizen's right under law and legal procedures.

54. A great portion of the laws and procedures are based upon the code systems of the civil law countries of Western Europe which were in turn based on Roman law.

55. On Taiwan, the tradition of a legal system is still carried on and the struggle for its full realization is not over. The principle of Rule by Law continues to be advocated by government, but the application of the laws in practice remains incomplete.

4

Law In Communist China

The ouster of the Kuomintang in 1949 and its replacement by the Communist regime marked the end
of Mainland China's first period of legal reform
and the beginning of a new and more intriguing
era. In studying Chinese Communist law we are
entering a highly speculative area, handicapped
both by the unavailability of source materials
and the recentness of events. Furthermore, the
Chinese Communists evidently have not themselves
charted a clear and definitive course for their
legal development.
     Marx and Lenin regarded law as an instrument
of state power designed to enforce the dominance
of the ruling class. Mao Tse-tung holds a similar
view of law and considers it an instrument of the
state for the realization of socialism and the
suppression of enemy classes. The Marxist dialec-
tic predicted the withering away of law together
with the state when classes were eliminated in a

pure Communist society. However, the Communist revolution of 1949 did not immediately achieve a classless society in China. During the transitional period there is a need for law; effective government and orderly society are impossible without some legal rules and enforcement.

After it seized power in 1949, the government of Communist China immediately abolished all the laws of the Nationalist government because they believed that those laws represented only the interest of the bourgeois class and feudal society. During the first few years, the Chinese laws, however, were not actually replaced by new codes, but by a mixture of statutes, rules, decrees, orders, Party regulations, and directives. Although some important statutes, such as Marriage Law, the Agrarian Reform Law, and the Electoral Law, had been enacted by the Communist government immediately after 1949, up to the time of this study, Communist China has not had yet a comprehensive civil or criminal code, nor a standard legal procedure. It is very unusual for a modern state to operate more than seventeen years without an established or codified law system. The Communist government explained that the incompleteness of the law system was largely due to the rigidity of the laws. They should not be enacted prematurely because of the continued political and economic developments in China. In other words, the legal system requires a certain stage of experimentation before the final codification.

In Communist China, the political policy of the Party is an integral part of the law. A great number of the laws are made by nongovernmental or political institutions, the Communist Party of China for example, which have no constitutional authority to make law. Political resolutions of the Party played a significant role in the application of law.[1]

Well-organized law courts were established from the very beginning of the Communist regime.

In addition to the people's courts, *Jen-ming tiao-che Wei-yuan-hui* or *People's Mediation Committees* and *People's Tribunals* were instituted to assist legal settlement of minor civil disputes and suppression of "reactionary" cases.[2] A court system is provided by the Constitution.[3] However, the law courts are designed to protect the interest of the state rather than being independent arbiters for the interests of the individuals. Theoretically, the Constitution of the People's Republic grants and protects many "fundamental" rights of the citizens,[4] but in practice, the legal system of Communist China does not acknowledge any individual right that is in conflict with the interests of the Communist state.[5]

The Chinese law system rejected Western legal principles, for example the concept of *nullum crimen sine lege* or "no crime without a law," the presumption of innocence,[6] and the free evaluation of evidence by the judge.[7] Crime by analogy is again commonly used by the judicial authorities.[8] In ordinary civil and criminal cases, the nature of the disputes or conflicts is largely private, between individuals of similar political, economic, and social background, and the courts are perhaps impartial and independent. But in cases involving "political crime" against the state or the Party, the judges are expected not only to hear and decide, but also to prosecute. Formal interference with judicial administration by the Party is ordinarily unnecessary because most, if not all, of the judges are members of the Party. Both legal and extralegal methods are used in liquidating those who are "reactionary" to the State.

Perhaps the most outstanding roles played by the law courts in Communist China, in addition to their judicial functions, are educational[9] and propaganda ones. The trial of a case in the presence of the masses enables the entire legal proceeding to serve educational and propaganda purposes. Forced labor rather than imprisonment is commonly used for punishment.[10] The government hopes not only to reform "socially undesirable" individuals through hard labor, but also to increase production.

The Office of the Procurator has always played a significant role in the modern Chinese legal system. In Communist China, procuratorate is a very influential branch of the judicial administration.[11] The main function of the procuratorate is to supervise the enforcement of law by the courts and administrative agencies. It has jurisdiction over all departments of the State Council, all local organs of the state, and all citizens. It serves as the State prosecutor and has the power to protest decisions of the courts. Politically speaking, the procuratorate is more important to the Party than the law courts.

We now shall turn to the development of law system in Communist China.

The Development of
Chinese Communist Law

After the "liberation" in May 1949, that is, the seizure of power by the army and the Communist Party, the people of the Chinese mainland learned gradually, by experience, what the new conception of law was. They expected new legislation, but little by little, they realized that the change was of a much more radical nature. The very foundation of the judicial system underwent an astonishing mutation. All the former codes were abolished and the law texts were abrogated without being replaced by others. In the course of the following years, there appeared only some "regulations", such as those dealing with political offences during the movement for the "suppression of counter-revolutionaries", a procedural rule, largely theoretical, the law on marriage and divorce, the law on agrarian reform, the law on elections, and certain texts on trade unions and cooperatives.

Undoubtedly, readers of Marx and Lenin could point out to the initiates what the new orientations might be, but the instruction of the masses in this regard was carried out in a much less theoretical manner, by action and practice. In this way, it was gradually understood that former laws were bourgeois, not so much by their content — which could have been modified — but by their very nature as legislative texts offering support to the persons in power. The new legal system was not to be hampered in its action for the benefit of the people by laws which might be invoked by an accused or a defendant as a means of self-protection. The government had to be completely free of juridical interference, because the new State aims only at the happiness of the masses, not the special classes. In this regard, the State, and even the most humble of its officials, is presupposed to be endowed with true infallibility. Consequently, former laws would result in a hampering of beneficient action by impeding adherence to the circumstances. Moreover, such a law might arm the individual and frustrate the omnipotence of the People's State. And this People's State, acting, by definition, in the spirit of the Revolution, must not be limited in any way whatsoever.

The person brought before justice is not to defend himself but to yield. To defend oneself constitutes a veritable revolt against governmental authority.[12] Finally, absolute obedience is due in the event of any indication, however slight it may be, of the will of the government. It is not necessary that this will of the government be laid down by legislative or statutory law.[13] The order of an ordinary local official need not be based on a law; it is law in itself because it is the voice of the government; it is a veritable source of law.

From 1949 to 1953, a period of economic reconstruction and political consolidation occurred roughly comparable to the period of War Communism in the Soviet Union (1917-1921). During this per-

iod the law of Communist China served as an instrument of terror, as the Party proceeded to re-
lentlessly crush all sources of political opposition. Although the Communist government created
a system of laws and courts, much criminal punishment was administered outside the law courts. In
many kinds of cases the police were authorized to
investigate, detain, prosecute, and convict. Military control commissions continued to administer
both legal and extralegal functions in large areas
of the country.

During the "mass movements" period of land
reform and counter-revolution elimination, ad hoc
"people's tribunals" were formed and administered
their own brand of justice. In order to relieve
the heavy case load of the courts, in the areas
of their jurisdiction basic people's courts may,
according to the size of the territory and population, establish people's tribunals. These tribunals are the component parts of the basic people's courts, and their judgments and orders are
the judgments and orders of the basic people's
courts.[14] The main function of these "people's
tribunals" was to conduct "mass trials." Hundreds
of thousands of class enemies were sentenced to
death or sent to long terms of "reform through
labor."[15] In short, during this first stage of
legal development, the army and the police served
as the legal instrument for oppressing counter-
revolutionary elements.

Beginning in the Spring of 1953, shortly after
the initiation of the First Five Year Plan for economic development, the government of Communist
China decided not only to adopt the Soviet economic model, but also to develop a legal system on
the Soviet pattern. By the end of 1954, this decision had resulted in the promulgation of a constitution and a series of laws that established
the framework of an orderly system for the administration of justice.[16] The system was similar
to that which was erected along European lines in

the Soviet Union during the relatively moderate
period of the New Economic Policy (1921-1928),
and which coexisted with a parallel system of
extrajudicial coercion.[17]

Under this new legal system, citizens were
protected against illegal detention, arrest, and
search.[18] The national procuracy was organized
shortly after the establishment of Communist government. It was authorized to exercise general
supervision over the legality of the action of
all government organs including the police.[19]
But, in practice its primary role has been that
of a reviewing rather than an initiating agency.
Implicit in the constitutional grant of judicial
power to the courts was the understanding that,
contrary to the situation that prevailed in the
Soviet Union until after Stalin's death, they
were designed exclusively as the agencies for the
adjudication of criminal cases.[20] The trials in
courts of the first instance were heard in public
by a judge and two people's assessors and the accused was entitled to offer a defence.[21] It was
contemplated that this defence would be made for
the defendant by the new "people's lawyers."[22]
In theory the people's courts were to be independent in administering justice, "subject only to
the law",[23] but in practice individual judges were
to serve at the pleasure of the executive or legislative decision-makers.[24]

During this period, rules of criminal procedure were made for experimental use before the
formal codification of a system of criminal law.
Many law school professors were called upon to
write texts that were both to guide the administration of justice during the "experimentation
period" and to assist the drafting of the law itself. This entire lawmaking effort was to be
undertaken with the assistance of Russian legal
experts, who had come to help the Chinese understand the Soviet codes, and many of these Soviet
laws were translated into Chinese. The official

61

attitude towards law was the same as it was towards other aspects of the Soviet experience — to adopt the advanced experiences of the Soviet Union to China's transitional conditions.[25]

These were not mere paper reforms, but radical political-legal reforms. A wave of terror, the movement to "eliminate counter-revolution", was instituted in late 1955. By copying Stalin's collectivization efforts of the late 1920s and early 1930s, the Communist government of China sought to prepare the ground for a rapid socialist transformation of agriculture and industry. But shortly after Khrushchev publicly launched his program of de-Stalinization in early 1956, an emphasis upon "legality" reappeared in China, and at least in the larger cities, such as Shanghai and Peking, implementation of many of the reform commenced.[26] The power of the police to detain, interrogate, and arrest began to follow the procedures that provided for more regularized internal checks in order to prevent arbitrary action by low level cadres. In some cases, the police did not always comply with the requirement of obtaining the procuratorate's permission before issuing an arrest warrant; nevertheless the procuratorate was usually able to carry out conscientiously its obligation to review police recommendations to prosecute.[27]

For the most part, adjudication continued, as in the past, to take place behind closed doors. The accused, without legal counsel, was subjected to judicial interrogation in an effort to verify the evidence provided by the investigating agencies. The nonlegal assessors who sat with the legally-trained judge in public trials were designed to display the participation of the masses in the administration of justice.[28] Innocence was not seriously at issue because, if pretrial judicial screening found proof of a crime to be insufficient, the case was not scheduled for public trial but was either dismissed or returned to the procuratorate or police for further investigation.[29]

The defendant often had a formal opportunity to confront his accusers when defence counsel performed his argument with spirit and ability for mitigation or for conviction of a lesser crime. These experiments, blended in the legal process, constituted morality plays that were carefully designed for the education and edification of the masses; later public trials were often authentic attempts at determining the degree of the defendant's guilt and the legal punishment.

The people's courts, which were almost entirely staffed by members of the Communist Party and its junior affiliate, the Communist Youth League, were, of course, entirely dependent on the Party.[30] Local Party officials frequently interfered with individual cases. In fact, they were often asked, as the new local "gentry", to serve as the non-legal "mediator" in civil disputes. Yet generally this was an era when the Party's will was carried out by means of Party control of the formulation of national judicial policies rather than by means of local Party control of actual decision making. The competence of the judiciary, most of the members having had little or no legal education, was gradually nourished during this period by the study of various laws, decrees, regulations, instructions, reports and selected cases that emanated from the Party; and by the series of law review articles and by the lectures that were originally delivered at the law schools and subsequently distributed. It was anticipated that enactment of the proposed criminal code that was before the National People's Congress in the Spring of 1957 would provide further substantial impetus to the reformation of the Chinese legal system in a direction similar to the Soviet law reform during the same period.

It is significant to note that at the end of this stage of law reform in May and early June, 1957, when Chairman Mao induced intellectuals to help "rectify" the Party by offering criticisms —

63

the movement of "let a hundred flowers bloom, let a hundred schools contend," — some law professors and legalists accused it, for example, of assuming a "nihilist standpoint towards law," of maintaining an attitude of superiority to the law, of committing serious violations of legality during past mass movements, of overstaffing the judiciary with ignorant Party members, and of obliterating the distinction between Party and government.[31] The criticisms apparently exceeded Mao Tse-tung's expectation and made it clear that intellectuals desired democratic reforms, including a more drastic reform of the criminal process in order to end the Party's monopoly of judicial power. The Party responded quickly. The response of the Party leaders was to initiate the "antirightist" movement that bitterly struck back at critics both inside and outside Party ranks.

The first casualty of the "antirightist" movement was a change in the system of administering the criminal law along the Soviet line of de-Stalinization. Chairman Mao and the Party had never felt comfortable about the importation of the formal Soviet legal system, which to them was essentially a Western pattern. As a result of the "hundred flowers", the Party leaders came to fear that the adoption of the entire Soviet system would consequently lead to the acceptance of bourgeois law and values. Therefore, during the second half of 1957 and in 1958, while de-Stalinization introduced a series of reforms that brought Soviet criminal law and procedure closer to the Western system,[32] in China principles of Western justice, such as the independence of the judiciary from political interference and the non-retroactivity of the criminal law, were severely denounced.[33]

Before we discuss the nature and characteristics of Chinese Communist law, it is inevitable and necessary to understand the legal theory. Since the legal system of Communist China has been profoundly influenced by the Soviet legal pattern, it is appropriate to discuss and anlayze the theoretical foundations of the Soviet conception of law prior to studying the legal theory of Communist China.

The Legal Theory of Communist China

The influence of Soviet concepts of law. To understand the Marxist theory of law, we must distinguish between society and State. "Bourgeois society", according to the Marxist definition, is the entity of those social relations which men enter unconsciously and under the delusion that they are acting on their free individual decisions, though the latter are objectively determined by the laws of political economy. State, on the other hand, implies compulsion exercised consciously for the sake of enforcing certain rules. Of these two fundamental aspects of human life, Hegel insists that the State is "the realization of morality" and, indeed, the supreme aim of human civilization, in sharpest contrast to the liberal theorists, for whom the State is at best a necessary evil, or rather an unreasonable police force interfering with the normal display of the laws of free competition. But both Marx and Hegel agree in assuming that there is a fundamental distinction between society and State. In this, Marx rejected the premise that the relations between these two aspects were dominated by the interference of the State in society.

The original contribution of Marxism to the dispute, apart from its rejection of the moral evaluation of such historical relationships, may be stated as follows: First, the basis of society is precisely described in terms of the mutual relations into which men enter for producing their material means of subsistence, and these relations are conditioned by the existing forces of production. Secondly, these social relations are described in terms of the prevailing economic structure of a given society. Thus, the attitudes of the individual members of this society are typified according to their relative positions in the socio-economic relationship, that is to say, their class position in the society. Thirdly, the general attitude of men towards social problems of any kind is tentatively explained in terms of class as the fundamental division of society. Thus, the history of mankind is explained as a history of class struggles. It follows that the state is to be regarded as dependent on society and class-division.

> The State is by no means a power imposed on society from without, just as little as it is "the reality of the moral idea", "the image and the reality of reason," as Hegel maintains. Rather, it is a product of society at a particular stage of development; it is the admission that this society has involved itself in insoluble self-contradictions and is cleft into irreconcilable antagonisms which it is powerless to excise. But in order that these antagonisms, classes with conflicting economic interests, shall not consume themselves and society in fruitless struggles, a power, apparently standing above society, has become necessary to moderate the conflict and keep it within the bounds of "order"; and this power, arisen out of Society, but placing itself above it and increasingly alienating itself from it, is the State...As the State arose from the need to keep class antagonisms in check, but, also, arose in the thick of the fight between the classes, it is normally the state of the most powerful, economically ruling class, which by its means becomes, also, the politically rul-

ing class and so acquires new means of holding down and exploiting the oppressed class.[34]

Marxism regards law, under modern conditions, as an emanation of the state. Law, as well as the state, is a historical phenomenon. It is a superstructure upon the economic basis of society, i.e., upon those relations which men enter in carrying on the social process of production. Property relations, for example, are merely legal expressions for existing relations of production, and social classes may be described as owning (or not owning) certain kinds of property. But legal and political forms of social consciousness must be distinguished from the underlying economic basis. Law can never be "higher" than the particular economic structure of society. It is certainly wrong to interpret Marxism by stating that the "superstructures", among them, law, reflect economic conditions automatically. Law not only reacts upon economics, but is also influenced by various forms of social consciousness even more remote from economic life than law itself, for example, by religious and philosophical conceptions.

The State, from which law emanates, is a product of the class struggle and is dominated by those classes responsible for social production. Therefore, law is bound to serve the economic interests of those classes.[35] In this sense, as long as there is a class society, there will be class justice: for the judges are simply doing their duty in preserving the existing order of society and by interpreting all ambiguous formulations of laws in conformity with their conception of the ultimate purpose of law. The use of the term *class justice*, in Marxist theory, is simply a way of describing the existing state and its law in terms of class, although the most frequent users of the term do so because they themselves are still bound by the ideologies upon which that law rests, and themselves believe in

67

the possibility of maintaining a classless legal system.[36]

The Marxist interpretation describes a general framework within which law evolves and has to work, and the way by which the coercive power of the state will secure the purposes of the society's class structure. But not all rules of behavior enforced by the state are necessary elements of that structure.[37] The basic difference between Marxist and any other idealist conception of law is not that Marx denies the importance of non-economic factors in determining the content of the law, but that he tries to investigate the historical, and ultimately the socio-economic origins of the human conceptions influencing law, and that he denies the ultimate validity of any of these conceptions.

Classical Marxism has influenced Soviet concepts of law mainly through Lenin's *State of Revolution*, written in the late Autumn, 1917, on the eve of the Bolshevist revolution. Lenin's theory of the law is, just as that of Marx and Engels, nothing else but an interpretation of the words of his masters.[38] As a result of this interpretation, Lenin states that in the phase of communist society, that is during the period of the proletarian dictatorship, there is still law, but this law is still to a certain degree "bourgeois" law:

> In the first phase of communist society (generally called socialism) "bourgeois law" is not abolished in its entirety, but only in part, only in proportion to the economic transformation so far attained, i.e., only in respect of the means of production. "Bourgeois law" recognizes them as the private property of separate individuals. Socialism converts them into common property. To that extent, and to that extent alone, does "bourgeois law" disappear.[39]

To the extent that bourgeois law disappears, the law assumes the character of socialist law.

Hence the law during the transitional period is at the same time bourgeois and socialist law. It is, to a certain extent, still bourgeois:

> It is "defect", says Marx, but it is unavoidable during the first phase of communism; for if we are not to fall into utopianism, we cannot imagine that, having overthrown capitalism, people will at once learn to work for society without any standards of law; indeed, the abolition of capitalism does not immediately lay the economic foundation for such a change — and there is no other standard yet than that of "bourgeois law". To this extent, therefore, a form of state is still necessary.[40]

In the first phase of communism, during the transition period of the proletarian dictatorship, there will be a law, for then a "standard of law" will still be necessary to induce people to work for society. A "standard" of law means exactly the same as a normative order, a system of norms.[41] The law, the observance of which is to be enforced by the State, can be only a system of norms, because only norms can be observed. Lenin considers the law of the Soviet state as normative order and does not regard it as a mere ideology. Lenin speaks of the law as a social reality and justifies its existence as a necessary means to induce people to work for society. His theory of law is by no means an illusive reflection of social reality. He continues: "Consequently, for a certain time not only bourgeois law but even the bourgeois state remains under communism without the bourgeoisie."[42] A "bourgeois state" and a "bourgeois law" without the bourgeoisie is a self-contradictory concept, for the bourgeois state is a coercive machine and the bourgeois law a coercive order, both for the purpose of maintaining the exploitation of the proletariat by the bourgeoisie. If there is no bourgeoisie, that is to say, no class exploiting another class, how could there be a coercive order for the purpose of maintaining exploitation?

According to the foregoing statements, the difference between the first and second stages of communism will be this: In the first stage the "bourgeois law" will disappear to a certain extent, whereas in the second stage it will disappear completely. In the first stage, the law is to a certain extent already socialist law. Will it be completely socialist law in the second stage? Lenin says that in the first stage of communism, the state does not wither away entirely, since there still remains the protection of "bourgeois law" which sanctifies actual inequality. Complete communism is necessary for the state to wither away completely. It is significant that Lenin does not refer to a complete withering away of law. Lenin's interpretation of Marx's doctrine does nothing to remove this ambiguity with respect to the future of law. Lenin does not say explicitly that there will be justice, but this notion is implied by his description of the transitional period. Following Marx, Lenin regards Western law, or bourgeois law, as a law of inequality. Although it pretends to be a law of equality, it is "really a violation of equality and an injustice." This implies that Lenin considers equality — true equality — as justice. Injustice is, according to Lenin, the meaning of Marx's interpretation of the "narrow horizon of bourgeois law" which is still characteristic of the law in the first stage of communism. This "narrow horizon of bourgeois law" compels one to calculate, with the hard-heartedness of a Shylock, whether one man has not worked half an hour more than another, whether or not he is getting less pay than another — this narrow horizon will then (in the second stage of communism) be left behind."[43] It means that in the final stage of communism there will be justice. Lenin says: "The first phase of communism, therefore,

still cannot produce justice and equality; differences, and unjust differences in wealth will
still exist."[44] This statement implies that the
second phase of communism will produce justice
and equality. Lenin explains further that, in
the first phase of communist society, the principle prevails: "He who does not work shall not
eat," and adds, "this socialist principle is already realized."[45] "For an equal quantity of
labor an equal quantity of products." This prin-
siple, too, is, according to Lenin, a socialist
principle, but not yet communism; and "bourgeois
law" — which gives to unequal individuals, in re-
turn for an unequal amount of work, an equal quantity of products — is not yet abolished. These
socialist principles already represent a certain
degree of justice, but not yet the highest degree,
which will be reached in the second phase of communism. In the first phase there will still be a
state, and "while the state exists, there is no
freedom. When there is freedom, there will be no
state."[46] In the second phase of sommunism, there
will be no state, and hence there will be freedom.
In this final stage of communism "the antagonism
between mental and physical labor disappears, that
is to say,...one of the principle sources of the
modern social inequality disappears."[47] Hence,
there will be true equality. That means the second phase of communism will be the realization of
the ideals of freedom and equality, and that means
the realization of justice.

There has been no fundamental disagreement between Soviet theorists as regards the definition
of law in general. The leading jurist, A. Y.
Vyshinsky, in an address delivered at the First
Congress on Problems of the Sciences of Soviet
State and Law (Moscow, 1938), outlined "the fundamental tasks of the science of Soviet Socialist
law."[48] One of the most characteristic features
of his theory of law is that it is openly and expressly presented as an effective instrument of

71

the policy of the Soviet government, directed at the abolition of capitalism and the realization of socialism. Vyshinsky says that:

> Over a period sufficiently (and unfortunately) long, the trend of our science of law has not been in accord with the interests of the cause of socialist building...Over a series of years a position almost of monopoly in legal science has been occupied by a group of persons who have turned out to be provocateurs and traitors — people who knew how actually to contrive the work of betraying our science, our state, and our fatherland under the mask of defending Marxism-Leninism and championing orthodox Marxism and the Marx-Lenin methodology.
> These persons directed their energies to holding back the development of our juridic thought and to perverting the essence of our Marx-Lenin doctrine concerning law and state. These persons strove to dash from the hands of the proletariat and the toilers of our land the Marx-Lenin doctrine of law and state which proved to be so potent an instrument in the struggle with the many bestial foes of socialism.[49]
> ...the legal science front still continues to lag behind the demands of our epoch — behind the demands of the party and of the government.[50]

According to Vyshinsky, who strictly follows the line laid down by Stalin, social science can be only Marxism. A political movement is presented as a scientific trend. Marxism, which is in the first place the political postulate to realize socialism, is at the same time science. Quoting Stalin, Vyshinsky says: "Marxism is the scientific expression of the deep-rooted and inherent interests of the worker class."[51] The interest of the worker class is socialism just as the interest of the bourgeois class is capitalism.

72

If science is socialism, then it is only consistent to expect a Soviet science of law to produce the norms of a socialist legal order. Stalin
said that science "knows how to create new traditions, new norms, new purposes."[52] Hence, Vyshinsky says:

> A theory of law is a system of legal princi-
> ples on the basis whereof the entire science
> of law — and all the branches of that science
> are built. Clearly the working out of these
> principles cannot have its inception in the norms
> of positive law: on the contrary, the norms of
> positive law — like all positive law as a
> whole — must be built in conformity with the
> principles established by a legal theory.[53]

The "theory of law" Vyshinsky has in mind is
evidently not a theory of positive law. It is a
theory which has to produce "legal principles".
But these legal principles are not the positive
law which is to be established on the basis of
these principles. If they are to be "legal" principles, they are legal not in the sense of positive law, but in the sense of norms of an ideal
law, the law that ought to be established in a
socialist society. It stands to reason that these
principles are the ideal norms of a socialist law.
According to Vyshinsky, one of the Soviet legalists most influential on the legal theory of Communist China, the "legal theory" which is that
"system of legal principles" on the basis of which
the positive law of the socialist state is to be
established, "rests on the principles of socialism
— that is, on the principles of the socialist revolution and of the socialist state and social order."[54] The normative principles, the ideal norms
of a socialist law, cannot be deduced by the
theory of law from the positive law. Where can
the theory of law find the normative principles on
the basis of which the right socialist law can be

established? Vyshinsky has the answer: He states that the principles of legal theory must be worked out from the beginning, not from law, but from life. A theory of law can therefore be built only upon the basis of the principles of the organization of social relationships which are explained in the final analysis by the production relationship, that is the basis of all the social relationships in any society.[55]

Since Vyshinsky takes it for granted that a true "science" of law can work out from life nothing else but the principles of socialist law, he comes to the conclusion:

> In posing the problem of the Marx-Lenin theory of law and state or, as it is called, the general theory of law and state — that is to say a theory of law and state which would provide a system of propositions based on principle and obligatory with reference to the direction and development of all legal science in its entirety and each of the specific juridic disciplines in particular — we have in view the principles which differentiate Soviet law from bourgeois law. The Soviet theory of law and state must afford a system of Soviet socialist principles which explain and are a condition of the *Socialist content* of Soviet juridic disciplines and juridic institutes.[56]

It explains that a theory of law *must* provide the principles of socialism as *obligatory* for the development of all legal science, which can mean only obligatory for all those who deal "scientifically" with problems of law. This is quite consistent with the notion of Marxism, which, denying the possibility of an objective, politically independent science, considers science as a mere ideological "superstructure" and, hence, as an instrument of politics. If a theory is wrong it must be anti-Marxist, and if it is anti-Marxist, it is unscientific. In *The Law of the Soviet State*, the leading Soviet legalist criticized those who declared that Soviet law was simply assimilated and adapted bourgeois law. Vyshinsky says that "the viciousness and pseudoscience of such theoretical propositions lie in their perversion of the fundamental principles of the Marxist-Leninist theory of law."[57] It is consistent with the fact that in the Marx-Engels doctrine state and law are inseparably connected with each other, the dogma of the withering away of the state in the course of the transition period could be applied, also, to the law. But, for political reasons, this view is no longer acceptable to the Soviet government. Vyshinsky maintains the utopian idea of a lawless society of future communism. In conformity with Stalin's reinterpretation of the Marx-Engels doctrine, he says: "Law — like the state — will wither away only in the highest phase of communism, with the annihilation of the capitalist encirclement."[58] Thus, the definition of the positive socialist Soviet law which the Institute of Law of the Academy of Science adopted is that:

> Law is the aggregate of the rules of conduct expressing the will of the dominant class and established in legal order, as well as customs and rules of community life confirmed by state authority, the application whereof is guaranteed by the coercive force of the state to the end of safeguarding, making secure and developing social relationships and arrangements advantageous and agreeable to the dominant class.[59]

Vyshinsky explains his definition of law as follows:

> Law is neither a system of social relationships nor a form of production relationships. Law is the aggregate of rules of conduct —

75

or norms: yet not of norms alone, but also of customs and rules of community living confirmed by state authority and coercively protected by that authority.[60]

According to the above statements, Vyshinsky's definition of the socialist Soviet law can be read as follows: Law is an aggregate of norms expressing the will of the ruling class, guaranteed by the coercive force of the State. This definition, however, applies only to the law of a society divided into two classes, dominant and dominated, and that means — according to the economic interpretation of society — an exploiting and an exploited class. But this was no longer the system of Soviet society, where, as the CPSU declared, there are no longer exploiters and exploited, where the means of production are owned by the people, and, therefore, there can be no dominant class. Vyshinsky seems quite aware of these inconsistencies. He finally abandons his definition of the law as the expression of the exclusive will of a dominant class; he declares that the Soviet law is the will of all the people of the Soviet state.[61]

Vyshinsky stated that socialist law during the transitional period from socialism to communism is a system of norms established by the legislation of the "toilers" and expressing the will of the whole Soviet people, led by the working classes headed by the Communist Party, in order to protect and to develop socialist relations and the building of a communist society.[62] This has been integrated into the definition of law by the Chinese Communists, which we shall discuss in the following pages.

Since Soviet law is a special type of law, the definition of law must be applicable to the Soviet law. According to the *Law of the Soviet State*, the Soviet law is

76

the aggregate of the rules of conduct established in the form of legislation by the authority of the toilers and expressive of their will. The effective operation of these rules is guaranteed by the entire coercive force of the socialist state in order to defend, to secure, and to develop relationships and arrangements advantageous and agreeable to the toilers, and completely and finally to annihilate capitalism and its remnants in the economic system, the way of life, and human consciousness — in order to build a communist society.[63]

The statement that the law is the expression of the will of the whole people, and not only of the will of that part which dominates over the others, means that the law guarantees the interests of all individuals whose behavior it regulates. Thus, it may be assumed that the law is in the interest of all people and, hence, in conformity with their will. This is a well-known formula of the ideological school of bourgeois jurisprudence.

But the statement that the law is the will of the entire people is an ideological fiction, whether it is used to justify capitalist or socialist law. For, if the law were really in conformity with the will of all, it would not need to have a coercive character. Such a social order could only be based on the voluntary obedience of its subjects, and, hence, there would be no law at all. This may be true in the perfect communism of the future; but it is certainly not true in the law system of the Soviet Union.

Justice has been claimed as a major aim by Bolsheviks since their seizure of power. They have argued that the principle of Western justice — independence of the judiciary from the legislative and executive branches of government, and the provision of a fair trial, are designed solely to mask the injustice of the Western law system.

Marx said that this justice was really only for the limited few who ruled. The state, according to his anlaysis, was an instrument of class domination; the laws were no more than instruments of a ruling class. Since law is the espression of the will of the ruling class and an instrument to maintain the interest of the ruling class, it could not be considered impartial.

Both the Soviets and the Chinese Communists have never claimed to administer justice in any abstract sense. They claimed that their law systems are more democratic than those in the West, because the socialist system of government represents the masses. They declare openly that their laws are the instruments of state policy and by no means impartial. In the earlier years of their regime, the Soviets spoke frequently and proudly of "revolutionary legality", by which they meant the maintenance of order for the benefit of the revolution. They denounced the concept of separation of powers so basic to the American system. In keeping with Marx's analysis, they have said that the separation claimed in the United States is merely theoretical and that American judges are as much subjected to the pressures of the political party in power and its instrument, the executive branch of government, as are the judges in their own system.

In view of the Soviet attitude toward law, and their insistence that judges be politically obligated in enforcing the policies of the Communist Party, one may wonder why the Soviet system includes courts at all. It is possible to imagine that an official of the Soviet Ministry of Justice could preside over a judicial dispute. There are several reasons why Soviet leaders have preferred to establish a body that they have called a "court" rather than to utilize administrators of the Ministry of Justice. First, Lenin inherited a society in which the court, in spite of Marx's criticism of its injustice, enjoyed considerable popular esteem. To have abandoned the concept of a court right after the revolution would have caused apprehension among the people. Perhaps that is why within a month after the revolution a decree established a new court system to replace the old. Ever since that time the court has been retained. Secondly, administrative efficiency is said to play a part in the decision. It has been found that the judicial function is a specialized one, requiring a greater measure of contemplation and more time to determine facts than is customary in an administrative agency. The denial of the separability of politics and law has meant to Soviet leaders that the judicial function was not separable from the administrative function. Soviet judges are admonished to study their politics carefully and to keep in constant touch with political leadership. They are not permitted to separate themselves from the policies of the Communist Party. In fact, over half of them at the lowest level, and all of them at the highest, are members of the Communist Party of the Soviet Union.[64] Finally, there can be no opposition in court to the policies of the Party.

All of these reasons are rationalized and accepted in the same manner under the legal system of Communist China.

Mao's Legal Theory

The guiding spirit of Chinese Communist law, which is merged with the law itself, is Maoism-Leninism-Marxism, in that order. Fully apprehensive of the danger inherent in a discrepancy between *fa* and the people's sense of justice, the Communist Party of China, renowned for its mass organizational ability, mobilized all the human resources at its disposal — Party members, cadres, and students — to remold public opinion into embracing the Communist li based on Mao Tse-tung's "New Democracy".

In considering the major characteristics of the legal system of Communist China, we must bear in mind the fact that its system is a product of many sources. A particularly strong influence from the Soviet Union as well as the indigenous Chinese conditions, both traditional and Communistic, can be demonstrated. That the Soviet law system, both legal theory and law code, exercised a profound influence over the Chinese is quite understandable. As the first communist state, the Soviet Union has had a judicial experience of more than forty years. By following its model, many mistakes which the Soviet Union had made through trial and error may not be repeated. Furthermore, its system, which witnessed the Soviet transformation from a backward agrarian and feudal society into a first rate industrial and military power, must have many things to commend it to a country like China, whose present economic condition and problems are quite similar to those which existed in Russia following the Bolshevik Revolution. But the Chinese Communist Party was the first among all communist parties to realize the principle that there are different roads to socialism and that each country ought to adopt communism to its own national history, custom, and need. The legal system is no exception.

One basic communist notion is the equating of ideology with politics. "What we are actually dealing with, then, as we examine the relationship of ideology and politics in Communist China, is nothing less than the fundamental apparatus of the regime: its programmatic objectives, the range of its operations and methods and techniques of leadership."[65] The Party utilizes both its highly disciplined quasi-military organization and its powerful weapon of revolution and control. The communist theory of statecraft is to manipulate social forces and engender social chaos for the purpose of acquiring political power. The instruments used to foment social upheaval include the army, the police and the courts. Mao Tse-tung has said: "The army, police, and courts of the state are instruments through which classes oppress classes. To the hostile classes, the State apparatus is the instrument of oppression. It is violent, and not 'benevolent'."[66]

The philosophical justification for the regulation of society is discussed by Chairman Mao:

"You are dictatorial." My dear sir, you are right, that is just what we are. All the experience the Chinese people have accumulated through several decades teaches us to enforce the people's democratic dictatorship, that is, to deprive the reactionaries of the right to speak and let the people alone have that right.[67]

The "people", Mao explains, "are the peasants, workers, and petty and national bourgeoisie. Under the leadership of the working class and the Communist Party, these classes unite to form their own State and elect their own government; enforce their dictatorship over the lackeys of imperialism — the landlord class and bureaucratic capitalist class, and the Kuomintang reactionaries..."[68] Professor Schwartz in his commentary on this essay explains appropriately: "Ultimately, the power of the class imputation rests with the Communist Party, and beneath all class criteria there lurks the very old criterion of support of, or opposition to, the State."[69] The legal organs play an important role in determining class status.

Communist China's attitude towards the position and function of socialist laws in the people's democratic dictatorship explains its theory of law:

Chairman Mao, Lenin and Marx all told us that law is the expression of the will of the ruling class, and the code of conduct formulated by political organizations of the state with the approval of the ruling class. Since law is the expression of the will of the ruling class and an instrument to maintain the interest of the ruling class, it is put into effect by the power of the state.[70]

Hence, according to the official instruction of the Central Committee of the Chinese Communist Party on Judiciary Reform,[71] law is a form of ideology enforced by the ruling class with force and compulsion. Thus, law is regarded as the product of class dictatorship, and its existence and execution are safeguarded by state power. The Communist leaders are convinced that the reason the feudalist law upheld the unlimited special privileges of the feudal lords over the peasants and right of slave owners "to slaughter their slaves at will," and why the capitalist law is used by the capitalist ruling class as "a whip against the proletariat and the working people is that the minority exploiting class was in control of the brutal force of class dictatorship."[72] Under the leadership of the Communist Party, Chinese people established the "people's democratic dictatorship." Consequently, "they are able to write laws through their own state agencies according to their own interest, and to use law as a weapon to suppress the resistance of the hostile class..."[73] In short, the socialist laws in China reflect the will of the working class and the broad masses of people.[74] These laws are to be enforced by the power of state and constitute a "weapon" for carrying out the "democratic dictatorship".

One of the basic notions in the legal philosophy of Communist China is that law transcends state power, and that law is the foundation of the state. They claimed that all laws are products of class dictatorship, enforced by the coercive power of the state. Thus, it is absolutely untrue to say that "Political power is born out of law," or

that "law restrains dictatorship." In answering
to the readers about the abolition of old legal
system, the New China News Agency pointed out:
"Any legal system, constitution, or law can only
be created by a class during the class struggle,
or after the seizure of political power by that
class. The type of constitution and the entire
legal system depends upon the nature of the political regime of the State."[75] Thus, socialist laws
are the products of proletarian revolution and
proletarian dictatorship. "It is not true to say
that law gives birth to revolution and dictatorship."[76] The legal theory of Communist China accepted Lenin's notion that dictatorship is a political system which owes its existence solely to
violent force, and is not restrained by any law.
That is to say, the revolutionary dictatorship of
the proletariat is a political regime established
and maintained through the use of violent force by
the proletariat against the bourgeoisie; it is a
regime not restrained by any law.[77] It is incon-
ceivable, according to Lenin as well as Mao Tse-
tung, that proletarian revolution and liberation
can succeed through regular activities according
to the existing law without using any violent
force. For law is only a means to promote and
"consolidate revolution"; it should never be an
obstacle to "proletarian dictatorship".

In September 1957, the Institute of Criminal
Law Research of the Central Political-Judicial
Cadres' School published a monograph, *The General
Principles of Criminal Law in the People's Republic of China*, which discusses and explains extensively the legal philosophy of Communist China.[78]
It begins with the warning that before studying
the socialist law of China, one must have a thorough understanding of the class character of
Chinese law. The only way to understand the
Chinese socialist law is "by exposing the historical sources of criminal law and by showing the
class character of offense and punishment and its

development according to the stand, viewpoint, and method of Marxism-Leninism,"[79] It claims that the law of the People's Republic is a branch of Marxist-Leninist jurisprudence. What is criminal law? It is, according to the official text, a branch of law, a product of the split of human society into classes and the formation of states. Following the formation of a state, the dominant class, in order to protect its class interest and ruling order, regulated those acts violating its interest and order by making them punishable crimes. Therefore, criminal law, according to the Chinese legal theory, is an instrument for the protection of a ruling class and is a weapon of the ruling class for the conduct of class struggle.[80]

The Chinese jurists agreed that, as a weapon of class struggle, criminal law, like the army, is used by the ruling class as a visible coercive force to "suppress its class enemies"; so that they will not resist or destroy the ruling order. It is a form of "state consciousness compulsorily and openly enforced by the ruling class with arms."[81] Through the entire history of China, the imperial dynasties, after seizing government power with military force, always took the enactment of law as their foremost task in order to suppress the resistance and to preserve their dominance. In ancient China, the so-called "law" was nothing but criminal code, because in those days *fa* (law) meant *hsing* (punishment),[82] and the *Imperial Law* was, in effect, criminal law.

Since criminal law is regarded as an instrument for the conduct of class struggle and its contents are characterized by the application of penalties to punish offenders, the nature of offense and the application of punishment are, therefore, always determined by the interest of the ruling class. It is agreed among both the Communist officials and academic scholars that criminal law is an expression of the will of the ruling class which seizes the government power of the

84

state. The contents of this will, however, are determined by the material conditions of existence of the ruling class. As Marx says in the *Manifesto of the Communist Party:* "...Just as your jurisprudence is but the will of your class made into a law for all, a will whose essential character and direction are determined by the economic condition of existence of your class."[83] Although this passage of Marx's dictum was aimed at the bourgeois law, undoubtedly its principle is applicable to all other laws in a class society.[84]

The legal theory of Communist China towards civil law can be found in the following passages:

> The civil law of the People's Republic of China is socialist civil law and the science of the civil law of the People's Republic of China is a branch of Marxist-Leninist jurisprudence. Under the leadership of the Communist Party of China, it has come into being and has developed through the constant evaluation of our activity in revolution and construction.[85]

Mao and his fellow jurists maintained, accepting the Marxist-Leninist legal notion completely, that both law and jurisprudence possess a very intensive class character and can only save the ruling class of a given period. Thus, China, as a revolutionaly regime, "does not recognize any other regime or law, nor any rule enacted by any other people."[86] Rather, "through the revolutionary struggle, the masses themselves directly create new law."[87]

The Chinese officials openly announced that the civil law of the People's Republic is socialist civil law, and is determined by China's socialist economic and political system. "It is an instrument of class struggle for the worker class who leads the vast masses of toiling people and fights for the complete realization of social-

85

ism."[88] The Communist Party regards that "the
civil law of China plays an important role in handling the people's internal contradictions."[89] The
Party also accepts the Soviet law as the model by
saying that "the socialist civil law is the Soviet
civil law. It is the first civil law in the history of mankind which can handle the people's internal contradictions."[90] The civil law, according to the legal theory of the People's Republic,
is the legal criterion for a common desire for the
completion of a socialist society rather than for
the resolution of basic conflict. For in socialist countries, "there is no conflict of basic interests among the people, nor between the state
and the toiling people..."[91] However, "if...the
national bourgeoisie have refused to accept our
policy, then the contradiction between the worker
class and the national bourgeoisie becomes the
contradiction between the enemy and ourselves."[92]
In short, law in Communist China is viewed as a
legal instrument to solve the "contradictions" between the national bourgeoisie and the proletariat
dictatorship. Law is not a technical term for the
standardization of social and economic behavior;
it is a regularization and codification of politics and policies.
It has been clearly expressed that:

The civil law of our Party and State is at the
service of the politics of our state. Since
the policies of our Party are the highest expression of the interests of the working class
and the toiling people, and the political
tasks of our State are, also, the common will
of the toiling people, the fact that the law
implements Party policies and serves politics
is a mark which shows that our country's law
expresses the will of the worker class and the
toiling people.[93]

Therefore, under the Chinese legal system, the
application of law and the execution of policies,

86

or the reliance on law and the implementation of political decisions, are entirely consistent with each other. In other words, lack of understanding of Party policies, or departure from the political line of the state, will make it impossible to apply the law. That means Party policy is "the soul of law, whereas law the concretization of Party policy"[94] and a tool for the realization of Party policy.

To sum up the above investigation, we may come to a conclusion that all laws, both civil and criminal, possess a very strong class character and Party character. It is the Maoist-Leninist-Marxist *science* of law which realistically serves as an effective instrument for the policies of the Party and "social justice" of the Chinese Communism.

In Communist China, Mao's ideology has been used as a major guidance both for law-making and law interpretation. In fact, the Chinese Communists mixed Mao's ideology with practically the entire law system.

The Role of Law — Legal
or Political

"A law is a political measure, it is politics."[95] With these words of Lenin, Communist China cemented its concept of a legal system. The judges and administrators brought to office after the seizure of power in 1949 were to frequently cite these words as justification for application of laws dictated by their consciences, even though they had no support for such action in the document in their hands with its inscription, "law," "decree" or "instruction".

The attitude that policy directives in the form of law were to be read for guidance, but were not binding, was encouraged by the events of the first three years following the revolution. Since the Communist Party had seized power in 1949 without a fully developed plan for the legal system it expected to establish, it authorized the men and women chosen to preserve order and settle disputes to utilize their "social consciences." Only a few key matters were made the subject of immediate legislation.[96]

In its program for a drastic and sweeping transformation of the economic and social order, the Communist government of China did not overlook the laws of the People's Republic, its court system, and the administration of justice as useful means for accomplishing its goals. Mme. Shih Liang, the non-communist Minister of Justice, reaffirmed the Maoist-Leninist-Marxist dogma concerning the role of law and courts, praised the "people's judicial system of New China" as "one of the fruits of the victory earned by the Chinese people...under the leadership of the Communist Party of China."[97] "Born of the people's revolutionary struggle," she said, "it is made to serve the people's revolutionary struggle..."[98]

For the attainment of its revolutionary goals, it has been stressed, the Chinese Communist regime finds it necessary to be able to wield virtually total control over the mass of the population. The law and court system of the country provides one more instrument through which the government can reach its political ends. The courts make no pretense of being impartial and independent. Instead, they are frankly "political" in nature, serving whatever policies and programs are decided by the party, and fulfilling whatever missions are assigned by it. In the words of the first President of the People's Supreme Court, Shen Chun-ju: "Our judicial work must serve political ends actively, and must be brought to bear on current central political tasks and mass movement."[99]

The "current tasks" to which President Shen was referring included that of suppressing "resolutely, sternly, and in good time all counterrevolutionary activities... and the resistance of the

88

reactionary classes," and protecting "the gains of land reform, production, reconstruction, and democratic order." These "political tasks" have been prescribed for the courts by the laws of the government as well. For example, Article 3 of the Provisional Regulations Governing the Organization of the People's Courts specifies that in trying criminal and civil cases, the courts are "to consolidate the people's democratic dictatorship, uphold the new democratic social order, and safeguard the fruit of the people's revolution..."[100] Earlier, the Provisional Regulations Governing the Organization of People's Courts also stated that these ad hoc judicial bodies were expected to protect revolutionary order and enforce governmental policies. What this practice of assigning political roles to the courts would mean for the concept of judicial independence and the tradition of a "government of laws, not men", was spelled out in blunt terms: "The law of the people's state is a weapon in the hands of the people to be used to punish subversive elements of all sorts, and is by no means something mysterious and abstruse to be controlled by a minority separated from the masses."[101]

In conformity with its aim of using the legal process as a powerful political instrument, one of the first actions of the new regime was the sweeping abrogation, under the Common Program, of all the legal codes of the previous Nationalist government. In the ensuing legal vacuum, certain basic documents and decrees were laid down by the Party leaders to serve as a stopgap legal system, and even Mao Tse-tung's 1940 essay, "On the New Democracy", was occasionally used as a basis for legal decisions.

Subsequently, the Communist regime showed no desire to give up this freedom of rule by enacting a wide range of detailed statutes and comprehensive codes, although it did set up a Law Codification Committee early in the spring of 1950 to prepare such codes. After sixteen years, the Party admitted that the laws of the country were still incomplete, but argued that there was no need for hurry in setting forth complete and detailed law codes which would be "neither mature nor urgently necessary." The Party officials rationalized this position by saying that legislation should proceed from the simple general principles to the complex detailed provisions, and that meanwhile the laws should be issued as needed, in accordance with the circumstantial problems. Whatever the rationalization, however, the fact remained that as long as such codes and detailed statutes were not on the books, the regime was free to legalize its every political whim and action and disregard of any limits that might otherwise have been imposed by judicial precedent or by the public opinion.

At the same time, the abrogation of all previous laws and the substitution of a few basic documents and decrees would have accomplished little to make the law system a useful too, unless the personnel staffing the courts were also amenable to political influences and willing to abandon completely their former standards for judging guilt and innocence in administering justice. The absence of judicial independence in the Chinese system is shown not only in the organizational structure but also in the absence of any power of judicial review on the part of the Supreme People's Court. Unlike the United States, for example, it has no power to declare a law or decree unconstitutional. Instead, the ultimate power of interpretation of law is reserved, under the 1954 Constitution, to the NPC and its Standing Committee — the body which also adopts or approves laws — as it was formerly reserved to the CPGC.

The Communists' reliance upon the judicial system as a political tool extends to the indirect as well as the direct consequences of court action. The court system carries out its political mission

90

directly by enforcing governmental reform policies and punishing the proclaimed enemies of the government. Indirectly, however, the system is also intended to have an educational effect upon the political attitudes of the masses. Mme. Shih, in her report to the GAC, stressed: "The people's courts are required not only to deal out punishment but also to educate the people. We must also conduct systematic propaganda-education on the ideas of law and the State in Marxism-Leninism and the Thought of Mao Tse-tung, in order to raise the quality of the cadres and educate the mases."[102] Her concluding sentence left no doubt about the political role of the law and court in Communist China: "only thus will it be possible for the people's judicial organs to become a genuinely powerful weapon of the people's democratic dictatorship."[103]

What was true in 1954 is still true today. Hence, it was not an exaggeration for an observer to conclude: "The People's Courts simply follow the direction and decision of the government and the Party officials and cadres. In the last analysis, the Communist dogma is the supreme law of the land and the Comunists are the final arbiters of right and wrong."[104]

NOTES

1. See Chapter 5.

2. See Chapter 6.

3. Article 73, The Constitution of the People's Republic of China, adopted by the First Session of the First National People's Congress in Peking, September 20, 1954. This Constitution defines the tasks of the Chinese Communist state in its transition to socialism and stipulates polit-

ical machinery for their execution. English text may be found in *People's China* (Peking), No. 19 (1954); Hsin-hua News Agency (NCNA), *Daily News Release* (DNR), September 1954; American Consulate General, Hong Kong, *Current Background,* No. 297 (October 5, 1954); Shao-chi Liu, *Report on the Draft Constitution of the People's Republic of China* (Peking: Foreign Language Press, 1954). Chinese text in *Hsueh-hsi (Study)* No. 10 (1954), pp. 3-14. Hereinafter cited as *The Constitution.*

4. The entire Chapter III of the *Constitution* is devoted to the "fundamental rights and duties of citizens."

5. For a concise and comprehensive analysis on the "Bill of Rights" of the Communist Chinese Constitution, see Franklin W. Houn, "Communist China's New Constitution," *The Western Political Quarterly* (June 1955), pp. 199-233.

6. See Yu-su Wu "Censure the Bourgeois Principle of Presumption of Innocence," *Cheng-fa yen-chiu* (Political-Legal Research), No. 2 (1958), pp. 37-41. Hereinafter cited as *Political-Legal Research.*

7. Tzu-pei Chang "Censure the Bourgeois Principle of the Judge's Free Evaluation of Evidence," *Political-Legal Research,* No. 2 (1958), pp. 42-48.

8. It was commonly used in the dynastic legal system before the modern law reform. See *supra,* pp. 38-39.

9. Discussed in Chapter VI.

10. See Chien Chang "Our Country's System of Education and Rehabilitation Through Labor." *Political-Legal Research,* No. 6 (1959), pp. 42-47.

11. The Chinese People's Procuratorates will be discussed separately in Chapter 6.

12. For example, a person, accused of having asked and received key money for renting a room in his house, attempted to explain to the judge that the tenant had simply accepted to pay for a trivial electrical repair. The judge flared up: to dare defend oneself constituted an attack on the government; did the accused believe himself still to be under the Kuomintang regime, etc. This case may provide some illustration of the general idea behind the legal system. *Hong Kong Times* (February 22, 1956).

13. The agrarian reform took place over a period of many months before the publication of the legal text which is supposed to govern the program.

14. Article 17, *Organic Law of the Courts.*

15. In Mao Tse-tung's famous speech of February 27, 1957, "On the Correct Handling of Contradictions Among the People," it reads: "The total number of those enemies of the people who were liquidated by our security forces numbers 800,000. This is the figure up to 1954." *The New York Times* (June 13, 1957), p. 8. Col. 5. Later, the Communist official published the text of the speech with an amended figure, "some" enemies of the people were sentenced to death. See *Chung-hua jen-min Kung-ho-kuo fa-kuei hui-pien (Compendium of Laws and Regulations of the People's Republic of China)*, Vol. 5, p. 13. Hereinafter cited as *FKHP*.

16. Those laws were: *Constitution of the People's Republic of China,* September 20, 1954; *Organic Law of the People's Courts of the People's Republic of China,* September 28, 1954; *Organic Law*

of the People's Procuratorates of the People's Republic of China, September 28, 1954; *Arrest and Detention Act,* December 20, 1954; *Act for the Organization of Public Security Stations,* December 31, 1954. All of these laws can be found in the *FKHP,* Vol I.

17. For the legal system in the Soviet Union during the period of New Economic Development, see John N. Hazard, *Settling Disputes in Soviet Society,* (New York: Columbia University Press, 1960).

18. See Articles 89, 90 of the Constitution; Articles 1-9 of the *Arrest and Detention Act;* note 16, *supra.*

19. See Articles 9, 11, 12 of the *Organic Law of the Procuratorates;* note 16, *supra.*

20. Article 73 of the Constitution; also see "Decision of the Standing Committee of the National People's Congress of the People's Republic of China Relating to Control of Counterrevolutionary Elements Uniformity — by Judgment of a People's Court," November 16, 1956, in the *FKHP,* Vol. 4, p. 246.

21. Article 76 of the *Constitution.*

22. For a detailed discussion on "people's lawyer", see chapter VI.

23. Article 78 of the *Constitution*; cf. Article 112 of the *Constitution of the Union of Soviet Socialist Republics* (1936).

24. See Article 28(4), 31(9) of the *Constitution.*

25. See Chih-jang Chang "The Fighting Mission of Our Courts and the Fighting Experience of the

Soviet Courts," *Political-Legal Research*, No. 1 (1954), p. 11; also, "Soviet Courts and Procuracy," *Political-Legal Research*, No. 4 (1954), pp. 29-35.

26. Ming Wang and Ch'un-liang, "How the People's Court of P'eng-lai ch'u, Shanghai Municipality, Learned (A Campaign of) Speeches on Law," *Fa-hsueh* (Science of Law), No. 8 (August 1958), p. 36. Hereinafter cited as *Science of Law*.

27. Chih-jang Chang "The People's Democratic Legal System of Our Country," *Political-Legal Research*, No. 6 (1956), pp. 4-8; see also Hsin-min Chou "The Nature and Tasks of the People's Procuratories," *Political-Legal Research*, No. 4 (1954), pp. 19-28.

28. Ya-tung Wang, "Judicial Work Must Resolutely Carry Out the Mass Line," *Science of Law*, No. 9 (September 1958), p. 11

29. For the investigating work, see W. C. Chao, "How Do the People's Procuratorates Do Their Investigation and Prosecution Work," *Science of Law*, No. 8 (October 1957), pp. 51-55.

30. See Ch'en Li-ping, "The Judicial Organs Must Resolutely Obey the Leadership of the Party," *Chun-chung* (The Masses), No. 8 (November 1958); also Ch'eng Chi-yung, "Following the Leadership of the Chinese Communist Party is the Basic Principle of the Organization and Activities of the State Organs," *Science of Law*, No. 6 (December 1957).

31. "We Must Create Conditions To (Let a Hundred Schools) Contend in Legal Studies," *Kuang Ming Daily* (June 12, 1957), Col. 1, p. 3.

32. The Soviet law reform has been evaluated with different opinions among the Western scholars. But all recognize the importance of such steps as

the abolition of Stalin's extrajudicial agencies for imposing severe criminal punishments, the increasing powers of the court and procuracy vis-à-vis the party controlled police, and the codification of criminal procedure. For a more detailed analysis on Soviet law reform, see Harold L. Berman, *Justice in the USSR: An Interpretation of Soviet Law* (Cambridge, Mass.: Harvard University Press, 1963), pp. 66-96.

33. See Wu Te-feng, "Struggle In Order To Defend the Socialist Legal System," *Political-Legal Research*, No. 1 (1958), pp. 10-17.

34. Friedrich Engels, *The Origin of Family, Private Property and the State* (London: Lawrence and Wishart, 1941), pp. 193-194.

35. *The Communist Manifesto of Karl Marx and Friedrich Engels*, ed. by D. Ryazanoff, (New York: Russell & Russell, 1963), p. 44.

36. See Chang Mou, "Through Separation from the Bourgeois Concept of Law," *Political-Legal Research*, No. 6 (1958), p. 33.

37. Harold Laski, *A Grammar of Politics* (London: G. Allen and Unwin, 1925), p. x.

38. Rudolf Schlesinger, *Soviet Legal Theory* (New York: Oxford University Press, 1945), p. 29.

39. V. I. Lenin, *State and Revolution* in his *Selected Works* (New York: International Publishers, 1937), Vol. VII, p. 224.

40. *Ibid*.

41. "As a norm, that is to say, as a specific meaning of human actions, the law exists as an idea

in the human mind or, to use the Marxian terminology, in the consciousness of men." See "The Law as Norm" in Hans Kelsen, *The Communist Theory of Law* (New York: Praeger, 1955), pp. 14-15.

42. Lenin, *State of Revolution,* p. 228.

43. Lenin, *State of Revolution,* p. 233.

44. *Ibid.*, p. 233.

45. *Ibid.*, p. 224.

46. *Ibid.*, p. 225

47. *Ibid.*, p. 225

48. Lenin, Stuchka, Reisner, Pashukanis, Stalin, Vyshinsky, Yudin, Golunskii, Strogovich, and Trainin, *Soviet Legal Philosophy,* tr. Hugh W. Babb, "The Twentieth Century Legal Philosophy Series," Vol. 5 (Cambridge, Mass.: Harvard University Press, 1951) p. 303.

49. *Soviet Legal Philosophy,* pp. 303-304.

50. *Ibid.*, p. 313.

51. *Ibid.*, p. 306.

52. *Ibid.*, p. 318.

53. *Ibid.*, p. 323.

54. *Ibid.*, p. 324.

55. *Ibid.*, p. 324. What is most amazing in this theory of the Bolshevik law is that it is exactly of the same type as that bourgeois theory — the natural law doctrine. Principles of law "from life," that is, from nature in general and from

the nature of society or social relationships in particular; with the only difference that these principles are the fundamental norms of capitalist law.

56. *Ibid.*, p. 324.

57. A. Y. Vyshinsky, *The Law of the Soviet State,* translated by Hugh W. Babb (New York: MacMillan, 1948), pp. 57-58.

58. *Ibid.*, p. 52.

59. *Soviet Legal Philosophy*, p. 336.

60. *Ibid.*, p. 337.

61. *Ibid.*, p. 339.

62. "Soviet Justice", quoted by Rudolf Schlesinger in *Soviet Legal Theory,* p. 243.

63. Vyshinsky, *The Law of the Soviet State,* p. 50.

64. See John N. Hazard, *The Soviet System of Government,* 3rd ed. (Chicago: University of Chicago Press, 1964), p. 170.

65. Arthur H. Steiner, "Ideology and Politics in Communist China," *The Annals of the American Academy of Political and Social Sciences* (January 1959), p. 30.

66. Mao Tse-tung, "On the People's Democratic Dictatorship," *Selected Works,* Vol. 5, (New York: International Publisher, 1962), p. 418.

67. *Ibid.*, p. 417.

68. *Ibid.*, pp. 417-418.

69. C. Brandt, B. Schwartz, and J. K. Fairbank, *A Documentary History of Chinese Communism* (Cambridge, Mass.: Harvard University Press, 1952), pp. 448-449.

70. Lu Chih and Chang Hao, "The Position and Function of Socialist Laws in People's Democratic Dictatorship," *Political-Legal Research,* No. 4 (1962), p. 26.

71. The Central Committee of the CPC on the Abolition of the Kuomintang Civil Code and on the Judicial Principles To Be Applied in Liberated Areas. Established in 1948.

72. Lu Chih, *op. cit.*, p. 27.

73. *Ibid.*

74. *Ibid.*

75. *People's Daily* (July 10, 1962).

76. *Ibid.*

77. V. I. Lenin, "Proletarian Revolution and Renegade Kautsky," *Complete Works of Lenin* (Peking: People's Press, 1956), Vol. 28, p. 218.

78. *Chung-hua Jen-min Kung-ho-kuo Hsing-fa Tsung-tse Chiang-i* (Peking: Legal Press, 1957). English translation by the Joint Publication Research Service (13331), March 1962. Hereinafter cited as *Principles of Criminal Law.*

79. *Principles of Criminal Law,* p. 3.

80. *Ibid.*

81. The "Instruction to Abolish the Six Codes of the Kuomintang and to Define the Judicial Prin-

ciples for the Liberated Area." Issued in 1949.
See also Ta-yin Wu, "The Nature and Characteristics of the Socialist Law," *Science of Law*, No. 3 (March 1958), p. 26.

82. See *supra*, pp. 17-18.

83. Quoted in S. C. Ho, "Marxist Theory of State and Law: In Commemoration of the 136th Birthday of Marx," *Political-Legal Research*, No. 1 (1954), p. 8.

84. *Ibid.*

85. *Basic Problems in the Civil Law of the People's Republic of China.* A monograph by The Central Political-Judicial Cadres' School (Peking, 1958). English translation by the U. S. Joint Publication Research Service (JPRS), No. 4879 (August 1961), p. 8. Hereinafter cited as *Basic Problems in the Civil Law*.

86. V. I. Lenin, *Selected Works of Lenin* (Peking: People's Press, 1954), p. 315.

87. *Ibid.*

88. *Basic Problems in Civil Law*, p. 12.

89. *Ibid.*, p. 13.

90. *Ibid.*

91. Mao Tse-tung, *On the Correct Handling the Internal Contradictions Among the People* (Peking: People's Press, 1957), p. 2.

92. *Ibid.*, p. 3.

93. *Basic Problems in Civil Law*, p. 16.

94. T. C. Chang, "Policy is the Soul of Law," *Political-Legal Research,* No. 3 (1958), p. 57.

95. V. I. Lenin, "Concerning a Caricature of Marxism and Concerning Imperialist Economism," *Collected Works* (4th ed. Moscow, 1946), p. 36.

96. Such as *Organic Law on the National People's Congress, Organic Laws on the People's Courts and the People's Procuratorates,* a *Trade Union Law,* a *Marriage Law,* an *Agrarian Reform Law, Regulations Governing the Punishment of Counter-Revolutionaries,* and *Regulations Against Corruption,* etc.

97. Statement made on commemorating the third anniversary of the People's Republic. *People's Daily* (September 23, 1952).

98. *Ibid.*

99. Speech made to the third session of the First National Committee of the CPPCC on October 28, 1951.

100. Text can be found in *Current Background,* No. 183 (May 26, 1952).

101. Editorial page in *People's Daily* (March 21, 1952).

102. In a joint directive of the Supreme People's Court and the Ministry of Justice "On Study and Implementation of Organic Law of People's Court," *People's Daily* December 11, 1954).

103. *Ibid.*

104. *The Orient* (Hong Kong), January 1964, p. 21.

5   The Nature of Chinese Socialist Law

Almost immediately after coming into power in 1949, the Communist Chinese government pronounced that "All laws, decrees and judicial systems of the Kuomintang reactionary government which oppress the people shall be abolished."[1] As a practical matter, this meant that "all the former texts were abrogated in mass."[2] To fill this vacuum, the Communist regime further provided that "law and decrees protecting the people shall be established."[3]

That was eighteen years ago. Many Kuomintang laws have yet to be replaced, leaving a vacuum in some areas of law. Are the existing laws adequate for China's needs? Are there any principles for the Chinese Communist legality? Are there sufficient legal sources for an understanding of the Communist Chinese legal system?

Western observers say "no." "Chinese law is in a trial-and-error period," declared one writer.

"It is impossible in China to refer to any legal abstracts or résumés."[4] Wrote another: "The Chinese juridical order cannot be described in the classical manner by an analysis of texts. Texts are few, and on many points, non-existent."[5] There is hardly any principle of legality in the Chinese legal system.

There are ample facts to support these observations. And the facts — more than stated admissions or explanations — indicate recognition on the part of the Communist Chinese legal experts themselves that their laws are truly inadequate. A Law Codification Committee was set up by the Peking government in the Spring of 1950; but still no formal civil law has been codified. "It is expected," wrote the Minister of Justice in 1957, "that the criminal code will be published and put in practice this year."[6] But after ten years, there is still no formal criminal code.

Serious criticism of the inadequacy of Chinese laws aroused during the so-called "Hundred Flowers" period — a time of *relative* political freedom in 1957. It was then that a number of liberal-minded Chinese jurists criticized the government's reluctance to produce complete codes. They pointed out that there were no basic laws for the people to rely upon. The few statutes in existence, they said, were full of extremely vague and sweeping provisions. Wu Chuan-yi, then a member of the Bureau of Law Codification, is reported to have characterized the existing laws as "exceedingly confused" and containing "hundreds of conflicting provisions." It was his conclusion that the absence of comprehensive enactments made it "difficult for the people to observe the present laws and principles of legality of the People's Republic."[7]

Even those who defend the delays in enacting formal laws and codes have admitted the inadequacy of Chinese law. Tung Pi-wu, former President of the Supreme People's Court, declared: "If we let the present situation of the incompletion of laws continue, or if we drag out the enactment process too long, there will be a serious problem."[8]

Tung likewise presented an "official" explanation for the absence of more comprehensive laws. He declared that the "people's democratic laws must not be prematurely, over-rigidly, and subjectively enacted."[9] Laws, he said, must be made to meet the "objective demand of political and economic development; therefore, the enactments must proceed from the simple to more complex provisions."[10] Wu Te-feng, Vice President of the Chinese Political Science and Law Association, also explained that "a time of rapid social change is not the time to codify laws. Law is the armor of the social system and it must change as the system changes...Besides, we prefer a gradually evolving system."[11]

Despite the absence of comprehensive codes, there is no doubt about the existence of some sort of legal system operating under the laws of the People's Republic. It is a system of law guided by the principle of socialist legality. One of the boasts of the Communist government, set forth in its leading propaganda magazine, is that "more people go to law than in the past... It is because justice in the old days was costly."[12] And there are at least 2,700 courts for them to go to.[13] Furthermore, there are a reported "4,000 odd laws and ordinances"[14] that can be applied by the courts.

There is in China a desire to have their law grow out of actual practice and real needs. But despite this emphasis by the Chinese on experimentation, it is clear that the broad lines of a legal apparatus have already been marked out. Since all laws of Communist China were based upon certain socialist legal norms, it is necessary to discuss briefly the principle of socialist legality before entering the character and contents of their laws.

The Principle of
Socialist Legality

The principle of legality is an essential characteristic of a state with enacted laws as postulated by nineteenth-century liberalism and subsequently put into effect. Such a state, acts through the law, on the basis of the law, and in accordance with the law. The legitimacy of any state activity also stems from the law, which is created by the representatives of the people and thus expresses the will of the people.

The raison d'etre of the principle of legality is that it effectively checks arbitrary action by state authorities even if it cannot prevent such action altogether. The resulting predictable response of legal machinery in all cases falling within the circumstances laid down by the law safeguards the legal protection of the individual. The guarantee that state action must be lawful is an element in such protection, which is itself one of the two universal factors in the concept of law (justice being the other).

As for the actual content of law, the principle of legality offers no criteria and remains quite neutral. It is an institution of law that subjects the activity of state authorities to certain restrictions and lays down the way in which it is to be carried out.[15]

Jurisprudence makes the distinction between material and formal legality. Material legality requires that the application of the law through administrative orders and decisions by the courts should correspond in their content to the appropriate statutory provisions.[16] Formal legality insists on observance of the legal enactment — constitution, statutes, and regulations.[17]

The principle of legality presupposes the existence of laws according to a comprehensive legal system. The extent to which observance of the principle of legality can make state activity predictable and strengthen the protection of the individual by the law is directly determined by the

by the legal limitations placed on state authorities, by clarity and compactness in the law and
the limits placed on governmental powers.

For a system of legality to be effective,
there must exist certain safeguards whereby the
legal aspects of the acts of one organ are subject to control by another. It is generally
agreed that the effectiveness of such control
depends on the independence of this other organ.
Thus, many countries have independent administrative courts to decide whether the acts of the
administration are lawful. In both civil and
criminal matters the decisions of lower courts
may be brought before higher courts. In countries
where the Rule of Law is fully applied, there are
constitutional courts to decide whether laws are
in accordance with the constitution.

In order to understand the content and scope
of Chinese socialist legality it may be useful
to review its evolution.

A period of revolutionary upheaval is naturally not conducive to legality, particularly when
the new regime sets out to transform the entire
social and legal structure. It has to be decided
what should be done with the old legal system,
since to set everything aside immediately would
leave a vacuum. As early as the "revolutionary
civil war" between 1924 and 1927, the Communist
Party of China expressed the "people's revolutionary legal consciousness" and prescribed principles
of socialist legality. Mao Tse-tung's "Inspection
Report on the Peasant Movement in Hunan" mentioned
the "fourteen great deeds," which include some of
the principles of socialist legality in civil law.[18]
The "First Peasant Congress of Hunan Province",
also adopted the "Resolution on the Judicial Problem" which explicitly stipulated: "All civil and
criminal laws are to be revised, and all those
provisions which are disadvantageous to the peasants are to be abolished."[19]

In February, 1949, the Chinese Communist government issued a decree on judicial procedure[20] stating that previous legislation should be applied provided it was not "contrary to the legal conscience of the workers", and ordered the people's courts to give decisions corresponding to their socialist legal conscience. It also expressed that all people's courts are prohibited from using any reference to statutes or judicial precedent from "pre-revolutionary" times. The courts were to be guided by the decrees of the workers' and peasants' government and the judges' own "socialist revolutionary conscience". Between 1950 and 1953, several important enactments of the Communist regime concerning such matters as marriage law, labor law, and agrarian law were already in force. The legal structure of the People's Republic was subsequently consolidated by means of the Constitution of 1954 in particular.

There was considerable discussion in party circles and among jurists to decide whether the government and the administration were bound by the new laws.[21] Mao's primary concern was that uniform legal rules should apply throughout the country. As he saw it, the principle of revolutionary legality was intended to ensure the obedience of the population and discipline in the ranks of the administration. In his interpretation of the concept of law, a leading Chinese jurist referred to Mao's dictum that: "Decrees are instructions appealing to general practical requirements...They should not be regarded as binding commands to be executed at all costs. We believe that the legal formula approximating most closely to Lenin's idea of the revolutionary decree is to regard it as an administrative instruction."[22] The principle of expediency fulfilled the same function of guiding the state activity as the general principles of law in Western countries. The Chinese socialist legality replaced these general principles of law with a concept that is entirely different in its class character — revolutionary expediency.[23]

Communist law similarly acknowledges to a greater or lesser degree most of the rules derived from the principle of legality, such as publication of laws before they come into force, clear and accessible compilation of the whole body of substantive and procedure law (codification), and prohibition of retroactive legislation. But, the operation of the principle of legality in Communist States is, nevertheless, circumscribed by distinct limits, which are of significance in both content and effect. To a certain extent, such limits spring naturally from the pattern of the communist state. Until the First National People's Congress, 1954 the constitutional form of the People's Republic of China was defined as the dictatorship of the proletariat. But, the new Constitution adopted by that Congress no longer uses the dictatorship of the working class as the only essential term and defines as "democratic state led by the working class and based on the alliance of workers and peasants."[24] The state is, now, the state of the "whole people", an organ to express the interests and the will of the "whole people".[25] This alteration in the Party's program is of purely terminological significance. Thus, Chinese legal scholars have stated that the state of the whole people and the state of the dictatorship of the proletariat belong to the same category, since they are of the same nature.[26]

There is nothing uncommon in the need to interpret the laws. This means that the effectiveness of the principle of legality is greatly dependent on the rules of interpretation. The measure of protection guaranteed by the lawful discharge of judicial or administrative functions can depend on the methods of interpretation that government authorities or courts use or have to use. Under a communist legal system, interpreta-

109

tion of the law depends in the final analysis on how the party chooses to interpret the law. It is the party's dictates that guide even the judge, whereas he would interpret the law according to his unbiased conviction.

The Interpretation
of Law

The interpretation of law is closely linked to the character of the law to be interpreted and the aims of any given legal system. Interpretation of laws relate to a whole system, and its sole aim is to prepare the way for correct decisions in the individual cases which arise when the law is put into practice. This gives particular importance to the dictates of unity and consistency among the various approaches to interpretation. A law cannot be considered in isolation. It has to be placed within a pattern of ideas, aims, and values. These are either stated in the law or in the higher authority of the constitution, or they stem from the extra-judicial rules such as moral conduct, good faith or social custom to which the law refers. In the administration of the law they must frequently be remodelled, with due regard for the circumstances they reflect, in order to cope with the vast range of problems emerging in new and unprecedented forms.

What then are the ideas, aims, and values by which those applying the law in Communist States are guided or have to let themselves be guided? In accordance with Soviet legal theory, Wu Ta-yin defines the aim of the socialist State and its law as follows: "The Socialist State and its law are the instruments for the achievement of socialist society and thereby of the standards of socialist social order."[27]

Knowledge of these repeatedly mentioned "laws of society" is acquired through the study of dia-

lectical and historical materialism. This doctrine
views human history as an inevitable natural process that occurs through a series of class struggles for domination of the economic basis of society and culminates in the creation of the classless and stateless society. The function of the
State and the law is to promote and accelerate
this evolutionary process. It is a vital element
in the pattern that only the Communist Party is
able to reveal the objective laws of this historical process and, therefore, to say how legislation and the application of the law can help to
accelerate the process in a given historical situation. It is the party which is equipped with
the scientific theory and carefully evaluates the
lessons of practical experience in order to discern the objective trends of reality and to direct and organize the devoted efforts of the popular masses on that basis.[28] The Communist Party
owns this monopoly on revolution in its capacity
as vanguard of the proletarian class, whose function as the most recent class to emerge in the
course of history is to eliminate class divisions
and to build the classless society.

Consequently, the so-called general line of
the Communist Party is of immense importance in
the administration and interpretation of the law.
It provides the basis for the all-important principle of "Partyness". The former President of
the Supreme People's Court of the People's Republic of China stressed the need for the courts
to apply this principle: "Judicial decisions
must reflect willingness to carry out the orders
of the Party of the working class and the Government."[29]

The principle of legality is no obstacle to
interpreting the laws on the basis of "Partyness".
Legality and "Partyness" are, in fact, in "dialectical unity". In the words of Ch'en Li-ping,
Deputy Minister of Justice, "to apply the law
according to 'Partyness' is to apply it in the

way which corresponds with the views of the majority of the workers and, therefore, with the aims
of the Party and the aims of the Government. But
it is at the same time to discern and put into
effect the dialectical unity of socialist legality and Communist 'Partyness'." This opinion is
in agreement with the view stated in the Soviet
Union that "Bolshevik 'Partyness' is the essence
of socialist legality."[30] A similar view stated
that:

> The decisions of the Central Committee of
> the Party of the working class always con-
> tain important guidance for all state or-
> gans; above all, they indicate very clearly
> to the organs of justice the most important
> areas to which they should devote their full
> attention at any particular time. Rapid im-
> plementation in the light of such indications
> is an important duty for all responsible mem-
> bers of the judiciary, and in particular jud-
> ges, attorneys, and notaries.[31]
>   In these decisions we, therefore, see not
> only general political indications. They con-
> stitute the basis for socialist legality which
> we must take within the judicial framework.[32]

The possibility of the new ruling class (the
working class) falling from power was ruled out,
but it was agreed that the economic situation had
not yet been moulded in a truly socialist pattern
and that class conflicts had not yet been entirely
overcome. There were still groups of the population that might hold up the natural process of
history. The principle of socialist legality,
therefore, demanded repressive action against elements that remained under the sway of bourgeois,
capitalist mental attitudes. "The remnants of
capitalist mentality in human consciousness" are
declared by communist theory to be responsible
for criminality, and in particular for offenses
against the property of state and society.

112

The above description of the principles and methods of legal interpretation, and in particular the way in which the party can affect policy, leads to the inescapable conclusion that the principle of legality can be used to make flexible adjustments of the law according to the specific demands of the state policy. Often, it was even the rule that party directives had precedence over the law so that it was "lawful" to violate the law in carrying them out. It is clearly demonstrated by Chinese legal theorists that judges should not hesitate to depart from the law and should show absolute obedience in following the Party's directives, which represented the highest rule for them.[33]

The way in which the party affects the government's and the administration's application of the law extends beyond the dominant role that its doctrine and resolutions play in legal interpretation by state authorities. Specific machinery has been set up for the party to supervise the administration.

The party has undisputed authority over the state administrative machinery, and this authority is in fact partly laid down in the party's constitution. It can be exercised in two directions: (1) either the party organ at a specific level of the hierarchy can issue a direct order to the administration at the corresponding level; or (2) so-called party cells are organized in the administrative authorities or their executive committees. Under the party's constitution, party cells have to be formed in all elected authorities containing three or more party members.[34] These party cells are required to ensure strict adherence to the decisions of the competent party organs in all matters to be dealt with by their respective authorities. They are responsible for seeing that all party orders are implemented by the authority in whose area the cells operate. This generally works out in practice by a member of the party cell stating

the party's attitude on a particular matter when
the authority meets, whereupon the authority
then makes whatever decision best corresponds
to the party's expressed desires.

The party also directs the executive authorities by means of the fusions of party and state
functions. The chairman or secretary of the executive committee of a municipal party will normally by the chairman of the executive committee
of the town's government.[35]

Although Article 78 of the Constitution states
that judges are independent and subject only to
the law, the courts are in fact basically subject
only to the party. "Our socialist justice is an
essential element in the State's over-all guidance,"[36] wrote Professor Chang, a member of the
Legal Advisory Council in Peking. He said that:

> In our State the courts function as part of
> the political machinery for guidance, and it
> has to be ensured by appropriate means that
> they are truly the instruments of the policy
> of the Communist Party and of the People's
> Government...The essential feature of ju-
> dicial policy is to implement Party and
> State policy in the form peculiar to judi-
> cial action and by means available to the
> judiciary...The Party's decisions have ab-
> solute binding force for all State officials
> and, therefore, for the judiciary also...[37]

Both in Communist China and the Soviet Union,
the courts follow the party's decisions in interpreting and administering the law. That their
independence is subject to this requirement was
indicated most clearly by the former Procurator-
General of the U.S.S.R.:

> We do not want to be thought to advocate
> judicial independence in its earlier forms.
> We believe the judiciary should be wholly

dependent on State policy and the representatives of the State. But, we wish to place the judiciary in a situation where their strict adherence to State policy and to no other can guarantee their being able to carry out that policy within the framework of the law and independently of extra-judicial factors.[38]

In states adhering to the Rule of Law on the western pattern, the principle of legality is concerned exclusively with the organs of the state. Parliaments are bound by the constitution in their legislative activities; both executive and judicial authorities must base their actions and decisions on the law and must act in accordance with the law. The whole purpose of the principle of legality is to offer private persons, their organizations, and undertakings protection against an excess or abuse of power by state authorities. Socialist legality is incomparably wider in the extent of its application to individuals. It commands universal allegiance, from every non-state organization and institution and from every private individual. In Communist China, as well as in other communist countries, socialist legality makes it the duty of the whole people not only to scrupulously observe the law but also to cooperate actively in *creating* socialist law, whose function is to give citizens a precise understanding of these "objective natural processes" of social evolution in order that they may organize all their essential individual activities in a "positive socialist society".

The principle of socialist legality is, therefore, an important instrument in the educational and cultural role of the socialist state, a vital tool in the gigantic task of reshaping man into a pattern that satisfies the demands of the stateless and classless communist society. Socialist legality demands that every single person should be imbued with knowledge of the laws of the socialist state and the rules of socialist community existence as well as the desire to follow those rules.

The courts have a leading role to play in the pursuit of this goal. The educational function of the ordinary courts is repeatedly emphasized in specific provisions of different branches of laws in both Communist China and the Soviet Union. For example, a Soviet principle of law states:

> By the whole of their activity, the courts educate the citizen of the U.S.S.R. in a spirit of devotion to the country and the Communist cause, in a spirit of strict and resolute observance of Soviet laws, in a spirit of respect for socialist property, of maintenance of labor discipline, of honest fulfillment of public and social tasks, of respect for the rights, honor, and dignity of citizens and for the rules of socialist community life.[39]

The educational role of the courts is even written into the law in Communist China.[40] The courts are required "to utilize their entire resources to educate the citizenry towards patriotism and a conscious respect for law."[41]

In the same way parties in a communist state guide the state's administrative activities, they determine the content of the law. The function of judicial law-making in Communist China, as well as in other communist states, is to implement the party line exactly by juridical methods. In Communist China, the normal legislative procedure is for acts, decrees, or ordinances to be drafted by the government, which is answerable to the Central Committee of the Party. After they have been agreed upon by the Central Committee, they are then turned into law by a state authority having legislative powers, namely the National People's

Congress,[42] or the State Council.[43] However, the Communist Party of China has also passed laws on its own, most commonly through ordinances issued by the Central Committee in conjunction with the State Council. This situation, which arises through the dominating role of the party, explains the principle of socialist legality. The Chinese Communist legality did not include the principle of formal legality — observance of the Rule of Law.

The Character and Function of Civil Law

On March 22, 1962, the Research Department of the Political and Law Association and the Editorial Board of *Cheng-fa Yen-Chiu* (Political-Legal Research), jointly, with several law schools in Peking and the Institute of Law of Academia Sinica, held a seminar on "The Character and Functions of Law in China during the Socialist Stage".[44]

At the meeting, views were exchanged and discussed. The process of these discussions shows that while participants held basically unanimous views on some basic problems concerning the nature and functions of law during the socialist stage in China, they held different views on the further analysis and elucidation of these problems. Most of them were law professors and agreed in the recognition of the class nature of Chinese law. There were four general characteristics in the nature of Chinese law: (1) it reflects the will of the ruling class, thus conforming with the basic interests of this class; (2) it is enacted by the state and has definite forms of written expression, such as law, ordinance, resolution, order, etc.; (3) it is a rule of conduct openly enforced by the coercive force of the ruling class; (4) it serves the dictatorship of the ruling class and is an effective instrument with which to realize class dictatorship.

The second view is that the concept of laws should embrace these three points: (1) it is the manifestation of the will of the ruling class; (2) it is the will of the State and is shown by organs of State power; (3) it is a scope of conduct with compulsion.

The third view is that law is the so-called state consciousness and pattern openly enforced by armed compulsion by the ruling class, which also explains the characteristic of law.

These three views are more or less the same and can be considered the majority view of those prominent Chinese legalists and law school professors. But there were, also, some divergent views in the seminar. For instance, concerning the specific expression of the will of the ruling class as reflected by Chinese law, a great many participants of the seminar suggested that this should express the will of the broad laboring people under the leadership of the working class. Some suggested that it may be even more thorough and correct if it is expressed as the will of the working class.

There were, also, different views concerning the function of law during the period of socialism. Professor Cheng Yu-yu, Director, Institute of Law, Academia Sinica, suggests that there should be two functions, namely: to resolve contradictions between the enemy and the people, and to settle internal contradictions among the people.[45] Others, led by Professor Chen Shou-i, Head of Law Department, Peking University, consider that law must have three basic functions: (1) to serve as a weapon in suppressing the enemies of the people, its main function being to resolve contradictions "between the enemy and ourselves"; (2) to serve as a supplementary tactic in persuasive education through its function of settling internal contradictions among the people; (3) to accelerate the growth of socialist economy through protection, recognition and adjustment of socialist economic relations.[46]

118

The question of whether law has compulsory functions among the people is one of the sharpest arguments among the Chinese Communist legalists and legal scholars. In general, there are three interpretations. One view is that Chinese socialist law has a strong compulsory function on the "enemy", but none on the people. The second view is that while it has great compulsory function on a few law violators, it has no such function on the majority of people who are self-consciously law-abiding. The third view is that while it has universal compulsory functions among the people, it has a compulsory function of an entirely different nature than dictatorship against the "enemy" of the people.

With these characters and functional concepts in mind, we shall proceed to take a closer look at the nature of the law of Communist China.

The civil law of the People's Republic is a branch of the overall socialist legal system of Communist China.[47] It is a cropus of statutes and rules governing certain property relations and personal non-property relations for the "realization of socialism".

Property relations, according to their interpretation, are the social relations which arise from the people's possession, control, exchange, and distribution of material wealth, namely economic relations.[48] These economic relations arise between state institutions, enterprises, cooperatives, social groups, and citizens. Certain property relations regulated by the civil law are part of these economic relations. They are: (1) the relation of property ownership; (2) certain exchange and distribution relations, mainly the exchange relations of equivalent benefits; and (3) the relation of property distribution after the death of a person. These property relations formed the three primary systems of the civil law of Communist China; namely, ownership, obligations, and succession.[49]

The civil law of China also governs certain personal non-property relations. These are the social relations which arise from some particular person's creation, possession, and control of certain "non-property" wealth. For instance, writings, invention relations, and the relations in the application of trade marks.[50] The personal non-property relations regulated by the civil law have the following characteristics: (1) such relations have the contents of "spiritual wealth"; for instance, the content of the relationship of of writing is a certain amount of work, and this is a sort of spiritual wealth, not material wealth;[51] (2) such spiritual wealth is closely connected with the identity of a particular person; for instance, a work always has its author, and therefore, the relationship of writings has its personal character or personal relationship;[52] (3) such relations are closely connected with the objects regulated by the civil law's property relations; for instance, the publication of a book brings in the relationship of payment for the work. It is precisely because of these facts that personal non-property relations are, also, included in the civil law.[53]

How does the civil law govern certain property relations and personal non-property relations? By governing, it means the separate treatment of different social relations according to the people's interest for the "construction of a socialist society". In other words, some treatments are for the purpose of consolidation and development, some for the purpose of restriction and prohibition. For example, property owned by all the people or the collective body must be consolidated and developed; unlawful acts obstructing the socialist economy and damaging the interests of others through the utilization of private property must be prohibited.[54] In explaining the role of the civil law, Tung Pi-wu, former President of the Supreme People's Court, stressed that although the

State makes the law, it can only be realized through the people's practical action.[55] He urges that citizens and social organizations strictly observe the rules of the civil law and "correctly exercise rights and perform duties in order to realize the governing role of the civil law in their daily life and consolidate the legal order of socialism."[56] The judgment of the court on civil disputes is a compulsory protection of the display of the role of civil law.

The various existing contradictions in social life may be saved by legal means and the political-economic roles of the party and the state. In the different periods of revolution, the conditions of contradiction existing in property and personal non-property relations, and the political-economic roles of the party, have decided the character and function of the civil law, during each of these periods.

During the transitional period — from the establishment of the People's Republic to the completion of the building of the nation into a socialist society — the general role of the party and the state is the gradual realization of the socialist industrialization and the socialist transformation of agriculture and capitalist industry and commerce. Thus, the basic function of the civil law is designed to realize the national economic plan and to advance the formation of the system of socialist ownership.

Between 1949 and 1952, the civil law of Communist China was primarily characterized by the elimination of "semi-feudal and semi-colonial" remnants in property relations, the abolition of land ownership by landlords,[57] the transformation of land ownership to peasants,[58] the extinction of feudal obligations,[59] the adjustment of industries and business through the unification of the economic-financial relations.[60] During this period China started using the order contract and other methods to make a preliminary reform of capitalist industry and commerce.[61]

In 1953, Communist China began to enter the stage of planned economic programs and more systematic reform of non-socialist sectors, and initiated the First Five Year Plan for the development of the national economy. During this state, the civil law concentrated mainly on the transformation of private ownership to public ownership. The following year, the People's Republic adopted its constitution,[62] and laid down the basic principles for the legislation of civil law. State and local governments also promulgated a series of statutory directives and orders in relation to the commercial needs.

In managing the socialist transformation of private to public ownership, peaceful means were used according to some written laws. For example, the Communist government did not adopt the method of compulsory confiscation to deprive the capitalists of their property.[63] They recognized the legal status of the capitalist enterprises under the civil law and granted them limited property ownership.[64] That means the method of "redemption" was used according to "principles of state capitalism".

By the latter part of 1955, the agricultural cooperativization movement came into full swing. The "Model Rules of the Agricultural Producers' Cooperative" adopted by the Standing Committee of the National People's Congress and the "Model Rules of the Advanced Agricultural Producers' Cooperative" adopted by the Third Conference of the National People's Congress included several civil laws which explicitly prescribed the legal status of the agricultural producers' cooperative and its property relations. They are the rules for the operation of the cooperative and the directives for the 500 million peasants.

For the purpose of the socialist transformation of capitalist industry and commerce, the Council of State on September 5, 1954 announced the "Provisional Regulations on State-Private Joint Industries and Enterprises", a law for state-private business co-ownership which Communist China called "state capitalism".[65] This act also provided for the legal rights and interests of private shareholders in such joint enterprises.[66] In early 1956, the Chinese government took a further step in the process of the socialist transformation of capitalist industry and commerce. A revised form of such joint management emerged, and a new system of fixed interest was introduced by the State Council[67] in order to provide some legal basis for the adjustment of property relations. All these statutory documents were promulgated as part of the civil law.[68] The resolution of the party pointed out that "since the socialist revolution has been basically completed, the main task of the state is to advance from the emancipation of productivity to the protection and development of productivity. We must further strengthen the legal system of the people's democracy and consolidate the order of socialist construction."[69] According to this particular period, the civil law should be concentrated on the protection of public ownership in China's planned socialist economy.

The principles of Chinese civil law are claimed as the reflection of the economic rules of socialism in law. That is to say, these economic rules of socialism are both the principles for the legislation of the civil law and fundamental criteria for the execution of law, the conduct of civil activities, and the means to solve civil disputes. If we take the Constitution of the People's Republic as the "supreme law of the land", we might find that the basic characters of the civil law are expressed in the following aspects.

The inviolability of the sanctity of public property and special protection for state property.[70] It is obvious that socialist public property is the result of the Communist revolution, and it is the material foundation for the further development of socialist society and, also, the source of state wealth and strength. For this reason, Article 101

123

of the Constitution prescribes: "The public property of the People's Republic of China is sacred
and inviolable. Protection and defence of public
property is the duty of every citizen." Since
state property is defined as property of "all the
people", the Constitution provides the development
of the state-operated economy with priority.[71]
This implies that special protection should be
given to state property as a part of public property.

The principle that public property is "sacred
and inviolable" is a legal principle peculiar to
socialist countries which are built on the foundation of public ownership. It is totally in
contrast to the legal principle of Western democ-
racies that private property is sacred and cannot be violated.

*The complete extinction of exploitation and
private ownership.*[72] It is widely believed that
the civil law of the People's Republic serves
primarily as the legal norm for this purpose.
With regard to capitalist industry and commerce,
the Constitution provides that capitalist ownership shall be "gradually replaced by the system
of ownership by the whole people".[73] This constitutional expression manifested the party's
policy of gradual "redemption for the bourgeoisie".
Between 1956 and 1964, the government issued a
good many legal directives and regulations concerning the socialist transformation of capitalist industry and commerce; and many of them became an important part of the civil law on property relations. Examples include the contract
for processing orders, the grant of legal status
to private enterprises, state-private joint enterprises, etc.

When the civil law regulated property relations involving peasants and handicraft industry
workers, it organized individual laborers through
the contract system. In addition, it provided
peasants and handicraft industry workers with

124

rules for the private means of production after they had joined the cooperatives, and promoted the transfer of small private ownership to collective public ownership. In short, the civil law is designed to prevent capitalism and private property ownership. But in practice, the state has been unable to implement this policy.

The realization of the national planned economy. The basic economic rules of socialism require that the national economy must be developed in accordance with a planned program. Without exception, the national economy of the People's Republic is a planned economy.[74] However, the realization of the state economic plan depends largely on the alteration of various property relations. Thus the civil law, with property relations as its main object, plays a significant role in the planned national economy.

The system of contracts in the civil law is one of the important instruments for the realization of the planned economy. Through the conclusion of contracts, it enables various business and corporations to join together according to plan and supervise one another. In the meantime, the civil law stipulates that the breaking of a contract will result in "penalty and compensation for the damage done". Thus, the civil law directs all business firms and corporations to perform their legal, or contractual obligations under the planned economic system.

One of the basic methods for operating and managing the socialist business under the planned economy is the system of "economic accounting". This system enables the private firms to function as independent businesses in the management of funds and the liability for loss of surplus on the one hand, and to decrease production costs and increase profits under the state plan on the other hand.[75] In other words, the system of "economic accounting" combines planning leadership of the state and financial self-responsibility of the firms. That means the state shares only the profits, not the loss. Thus, the civil law functioned as an effective legal force which regulates ownership relations and contractual obligations of the economic system of Communist China.

Equality of the citizen's civil rights and duties. The Constitution of 1954 provides: "All citizens of the People's Republic of China are equal before the law."[76] The rights and duties of individual citizens according to the Constitution, are all equal regardless of nationality, race, and sex.[77] At the same time, in Communist China, individual rights and duties are integrated. In other words, a citizen must perform his duties while enjoying his rights. This is a clear expression of the integration of individual interests with social public interests. As the President of the People's Republic stressed, "equal duty" is the vitally important supplement to bourgeois-democratic equal rights for the people of Communist China.[78] The equality of civil rights and duties implies, at least theoretically, the equality of the citizens' legal status in civil matters. Thus, "the principle of willingness" is included in the civil law of Communist China. "It is fundamentally different from the principle of 'freedom of contract' in the capitalist civil law."[79] It further expalins that the Chinese Communist system does not allow an individual to "freely impose his own will on the other party, or to curtail the interests of another person or social public interests for his personal interests."[80] For this purpose, freedoms which contrast with public interest are "naturally prohibited."[81]

Integration of individual interests and social public interests. Under the Communist system, individual interests and social public interests are closely integrated. The govern-

126

ment tells the people that their individual interests are inseparable from the increase of state wealth. The justification is that only by giving full protection to public interests can the individual be secure for his personal interests. The Constitution provides that the state prohibits the damaging of public interests with any private property.[82] As one of the major aspects of the civil law, this constitutional provision can be interpreted that state property should be protected with priority. The citizen, when possessing the ownership of his own property, must subject himself to the public interests. Any juristic act that violates public interests is void.

The government argues that while giving full protection to public interests, the state also extends its protection to the individual interests. For example, the law grants the citizen the means of life,[83] the right of succession to property,[84] and the right to participate in civil activities.

Among the socialist principles of Chinese civil law, we found that the center of attention lies in the protection of public ownership. Because it is strongly believed that only by doing so can the restoration of capitalism be prevented, the collective interests of Chinese socialism and the planned economic system be maintained. But in practice, the application of these principles of civil law contains a high degree of flexibility. That is to say, the characters and principles of the civil law are mitigated by the political conditions and party policies. All judicial staff and cadres are trained and indoctrinated in how to apply the principles of civil law, without being fictitious and abstract, to the political reality. In other words, when they apply the basic principles of the civil law to the practice of civil trials, they ought to be realistic in people's civil disputes.

The Marriage Law

Within the legal framework of Communist China, the Marriage Law is one of the most important "formal" civil laws.[85] The Marriage Law has become a show-piece of the Communist Chinese civil law. No other law has been publicized as much,[86] and perhaps no other law has been needed as much[87].

When the law on marriage was being drafted in 1949, some members of the party recommended delay. "Though the law may be promulgated;" they said, "its operation may be temporarily postponed. It may, then, be put into effect after a period of discussion is first given to the broad masses of the people."[88] But, Mao Tse-tung disagreed. "The Marriage Law," said Mao, "is only next in importance to the Fundamental Law (the Common Programme)....However, the idea of temporarily postponing its operation cannot be accepted."[89]

The abolition of the feudal marriage system and the introduction of a new marriage system on the basis of "New Democracy" is the fundamental principle of the Marriage Law of the People's Republic. It begins in these words: "The feudal marriage system which is based on arbitrary and compulsory arrangements and the superiority of man over woman and ignores the children's interests shall be abolished. The New Democratic marriage system, which is based on the free choice of partners, on monogamy, on equal rights for both sexes, and on the protection of the lawful interests of women and children, shall be put into effect."[90] "Bigamy, concubinage, child betrothal, interference with the remarriage of widows, and the exaction of money or gifts in connection with marriages, shall be prohibited."[91]

The Chinese Communists claimed that the chief aim of the Marriage Law is "to set Chinese women free from the bondage imposed upon them by the old system, ensure equality between husband and wife, promote their mutual aid, love...."[92] They

128

believe that it serves as an important guarantee for social emancipation and paves the way for the healthy development of the future generations.

Under the new law, the process of registration made marriage a modernized civil matter instead of a canonical contract, or a li marriage of the Chinese tradition. The cadres in the Registries and the officers in Local People's Government offices are fully empowered to issue or withhold marriage certificates.[93] And, registration with the Government is the condition of legitimacy.

Article 8 of the Law provides: "Husband and wife are in duty bound to love, respect, assist and look after each other, to live in harmony, to labor for production, to care for children, and to strive jointly for the welfare of the family, and the building up of a new society." It seems that People's Government does not regard marriage problems as private affairs, but as the public affairs of the members of the society. It is most noteworthy that the Law even made human love a duty. It appears like canon law, as Professor Vali accurately commented,[94] or a Communist li rather than a civil law.

The most important right of husband and wife according to this Law is "the right to free choice of occupation and free participation in work or in social activities."[95] This provision is in line with the consideration of the married couple as "companions", not bound by fidelity, domesticity, etc.

It is a direct paraphrase of the Soviet law that: "Persons violating this Law shall be punished in accordance with law. In cases where interference with the freedom of marriage has caused death or injury, the person guilty of such interference shall bear responsibility for the crime (criminal charge) before the law."[96]

However, the major criticism of the Marriage Law was "nothing new",[97] since bigamy, concubinage, child betrothal, an enumerated in Article 2 of the Marriage Law were crimes under the Nationalist Criminal Code. But, these inequalities and impediments in marriages were largely unenforced before the Communist government. Furthermore, the Marriage Law of the People's Republic confuses public duties with private duties, morality with law.

The Application of
the Civil Law

There is a strong emphasis on the realistic aspects of all the laws and statutes in Communist China applicable to the daily life of the people. In traditional Chinese society, people had never been accustomed to law and courts. Li rather than law was the criteria for individual behavior. Law is greatly emphasized in Communist China today as the criteria for action and measure of conduct. The legal system is primarily designed to cultivate the "legal mind" of the masses, and to educate them to rely upon their "self-consciousness to observe the law" in order that the law will become the *Communist li* for people's economic and social life. Whether the masses behave in accordance with the norms of law is a question of observance, whereas the effective enforcement of law or correct execution of law by the authorities is a question of application.

The application of the civil law is, then, the solution and judgment of civil cases through the application of the rules of civil law by courts and other state administrative agencies.[98] The civil law we discuss here refers not to any civil codes but to the civil statutes and decrees enacted by the National People's Congress or the Standing Committee of the NPC and promulgated by the Chairman of the People's Republic, and the documents and directives of civil rules issued by the State administrative authorities.[99]

130

The doctrine that "facts are the basis and law is the criterion" is the principle of dialectical materialism which has been closely observed in the application of law. Since law is regarded as the central expression of the will of the ruling class, the application of law is the "realization of the will of the ruling class" to solve disputes existing in social relations on the basis of facts.[100] Insofar as the Chinese civil law is concerned, it is the norm of human behavior enacted by the ruling class for the adjustment of certain social relations. It also may be regarded as the civil policy of the Communist Party. It explicitly prescribes individual conduct and behavior, what is lawful and what is unlawful. Thus, it is a pattern of new Chinese li, or may be better termed as Communist li.

In the application of law, the members of the judicial branch are required to have a good comprehension of the significance of law according to the policy of the party.[101] The following passages explain the "Principles" in the application of law taught in the Central Political-Judicial Cadres' School:

First, we must take the position of the worker class and use the method of class analysis in the application of law. Law is an expression of the will of the ruling class, an instrument of the ruling class for the purpose of class struggle and the adjustment of class relations. It expresses the ideology and policy of the ruling class. The legal theory and system of the bourgeoisie can only be idealistic and metaphysical. Our law, however, is the pragmatic and empirical which builds up socialism and communism. It is a manifestation of the world outlook of dialectical materialism in legal problems. It possesses an intense class character

and Party character and concretely expresses the viewpoint of the worker class.
Therefore, judicial workers will not be
able to comprehend and apply the rules of
law to safeguard socialist construction
and the legal rights and interests of
the citizen without taking the position
of the worker class, a materialistic
viewpoint, and the dialectical method.[102]

This statement expalins that law is general
while the case to be determined by law is specific; to reduce a general phenomenon to a specific
phenomenon requires judgment.[103] Communist China
believes that the only correct way of passing
legal judgment is through the method of class
analysis.

In criticising non-communist law it states
that:

The bourgeoise rightists hold that we
have placed too much emphasis on class
character, and therefore, our law is
narrow-minded.... Is the judiciary of
the bourgeoisie really just, impartial,
and supernatural in the application of
law? Marx, in his "Debate before the
Sixth Conference of Rhine Province",
offered an answer to this question.
"It is a foolish and unrealistic illusion to think that there will be an
impartial judiciary under a partial
legislature. Since law is selfish, then,
what is the real significance of impartial judgment? The judiciary can only
express the selfishness of the law and
unconditionally enforce it. This fully
explains that the bourgeois judiciary
is profoundly influenced by the character of the bourgeoisie, and they can
never apply law from a supernatural

stand without partiality. Only the judicial system of the worker class is impartial. Because they use the method of
class analysis to distinguish the enemy
from ourselves, wrong from right among
the people's internal disputes, apply
dictatorship to the enemy, and protect
the legal rights and interests of the
people....[104]

In Communist China, all the cadres for work
in the judiciary are also indoctrinated that the
norms of law must be "correctly carried out
through the complexity of real life" according
to the current political-economic situation with
the policy of the party as a guide. They are
told that law is a part of politics and is to
serve politics. It is the regularization and
formulation of party policy and an important
instrument for the realization of party policy.
The inseparable relationship between law and
policy requires that the Chinese judiciary must
be realistic in the application of law and sub-
ordinate law to politics.[105] In other words, the
entire legal system relies totally on the leadership of the party and its policy. It is admitted
bluntly that if law cannot be replaced by policy,
then the policy of the Party cannot be brought up
to the masses to guide their revolutionary activities before it is enacted into law through
legislation; and the political relationship between the Party and the masses will, thus, be cut
off.[106] Furthermore, if law cannot be replaced
by policy and the policy of the party cannot be
used as the guiding principle in the application
of law, then the judiciary can only subject itself to law but not the leadership of the party;
and consequently, it will become an independent
"kingdom" and its role in the dictatorship of the
people's democracy will not, thus, be functioned.[107]

Validity of the civil law in terms of time.
It is interesting to note that the application of
the civil law in Communist China requires a clear
understanding of the validity of the civil law in
terms of time, space, and persons. In other words,
there are differences of when, where, to whom, and
to what type of social relations the civil law
should be applied.

When the civil law comes into force and dis-
plays its governing role in certain social relations, it is a question of the validity of the
civil law in terms of time. The date of the promulgation of a law and the date of its enforcement
are sometimes in agreement with each other; i.e.,
it comes into force from the date of its promulgation. However, at other times, it does not.
For example, Article 18 of the Act for Compulsory
Insurance for Railway Passengers' Accidental In-
juries provides that "This Act will come into
force two months after the date of its promulgation."[108] In case the date of promulgation of a
law is not in conformity with the date of enforcement, it becomes effective on the date of the
latter.

Whether the law is retroactive depends solely
on the will of the ruling class. A great deal of
Chinese civil law which expressly stated that it
is retroactive on civil activities conducted before its promulgation. For example, the Agrarian
Reform Law[109] states, "The land ownership system
of feudal exploitation by the landlord class shall
be abolished, and the system of peasant land ownership shall be introduced...."[110] If the retroactive rules are not expressly provided in the law,
the rules of the new civil law are not applicable
to the civil relations existing before the promulgation of the law.

Territorial validity of the civil law. The
civil law of Communist China has legal effectiveness throughout the entire nation. But, the mag-
nitude of the Chinese mainland is so great that

the political-economic development in various areas is not balanced and customs are not at all in uniformity. The Constitution thus prescribes that the local people's congresses may "adopt and issue decisions with the limits of their authority as prescribed by law."[111] The governments of various autonomous regions, autonomous *chou* (nationality), and autonomous *hsien* (county) may also legislate statutes and laws suitable to the political, economic, and cultural characteristics of the nationalities. These laws are, of course, subject to the approval of the Standing Committee of the National People's Congress.[112] For example, the Marriage Law provides that in areas of national minorities, the people's government on the provincial level may enact certain modifications or supplementary statutes in regard to marriage.[113] In Communist China, any local legal rule is only effective in the administrative region of a given local people's council. Laws of one locality may only serve as a reference for the enactment of laws in another locality. However, they cannot be used directly as a legal basis or precedent for their judgments even when no such national statute was available and when their own localities had no corresponding legal rules. Any such judgment is considered as a violation of the law and is not in conformity with the principles of Chinese legal systems.[114]

Since the backgrounds and conditions of various localities are different, the legal regulations of one province may be in conflict with the laws of another. For instance, the interest rate in some national minority areas is higher than in other areas. A and B (national minority) signed a loan contract in A's territory. According to local laws, the interest of the loan did not exceed the regulated maximum rate, and the contract was lawful. After this credit transaction legally signed, both A and B came to Peking on business and got into a dispute because of the payment of the loan. If according to the laws of Peking, their agreed interest rate had exceeded the maximum rate, their cash should accordingly have been handled as a matter of usury. Then, the question arose whether the trial court should apply the law of the place where the court was located in hearing the case or the law under which the contract was signed. Since the loan contract between A and B was not in violation of the local statutes of the town in which the court was located, it was proper to apply the local law where the contract was signed to this juristic relation.[115]

Validity of the civil law in terms of persons. The civil law of Communist China has absolute power of command over the citizen "regardless of race, sex, age, class origin, and religion".[116] The civil law is also applicable to a juridical person.[117] Although both the citizen and the juridical person are the subjects of civil juristic relations, the nature of these two subjects is different. Some of the rules in the civil law are only applicable to the citizen and not the juridical person,[118] and vice versa.[119]

Foreigners in the territory of the People's Republic are classified into two groups: foreign diplomats and non-diplomats. The Provisional Regulations Governing Special Treatment of Foreign Diplomats and Consuls expressed that "foreign diplomats are immune from Chinese criminal and civil trials."[120] In other words, foreign diplomats in Communist China do enjoy diplomatic immunity and are exempted from both criminal and civil trials of the country in which they reside. If they are involved in civil disputes in China, these disputes are normally to be solved through diplomatic channels, and Chinese People's courts have no jurisdiction over them.[121] However, should a foreign diplomat file a civil suit in which he himself is a plaintiff, or should he accept the court's ruling, the court may then hear and pass judgment on such a civil dispute.

Chinese Communists accepted that diplomatic immunity is the international custom and the principle of equality and reciprocity. They certainly hope that their diplomats would enjoy the same immunity abroad. If they are involved in civil disputes in foreign countries, the rules of Chinese civil law are applied. They said that "diplomatic immunity is a matter of protocol in international relations. It does not necessarily affect the uniformity and independence of Chinese legal sovereignty."[122]

Aliens residing in Communist China are subject to the rules of the civil law. In civil cases involving foreigners, the People's courts do sometimes take their laws into consideration. This, however, does not mean that foreign law comes into force in the court's decisions. It merely applies some foreign laws as references into the Chinese civil law.[123]

Interpretation of the civil law. Under the Chinese law system interpretation of the civil law is one of the formal instruments for the development of jurisprudence. The power of law-making and the power to interpret the law are not separated in Communist China. The institutions having the power to interpret civil law are the National People's Congress, the Standing Committee of the National People's Congress, and other authorities that have power to enact civil statutes.[124] In trials, the Judicial Committee of the Supreme Court has power to interpret the civil law.[125] The people's courts at various levels, in hearing cases, may also interpret the meaning of the civil law according to their own understanding of the law rather than legal precedents.[126] However, such interpretation has its binding effect on parties only when the judgment of the court comes into legal force. It has no universal application.

137

The interpretation of law itself also possesses compulsory force.[127]

According to the nature of the power, we may classify the interpretation of the civil law into two major categories:

1. *Legislative interpretation*. The interpretation of law or statutes by those organs that have power to enact law or statutes is called legislative interpretation. In Communist China, when a law is promulgated, it is usually accompanied by a draft report of the law which explains the drafting procedure and legislative background. The purpose of a draft report is to educate the people to understand the "spirit of the law", and, furthermore, it is an official legislative interpretation which has universal binding force.[128] It is interesting to note that those governmental organs that have authority to enact statutory orders and directives also have power to interpret them if ambiguities arise during the execution of these statutes.

2. *Judicial Interpretation*. In the judicial process, when there is doubt as to which law is to be applied, and when the application of the law is made by the Supreme People's Court, judicial interpretation is then required. It not only has binding force over the lower courts, but over any person who is involved in this interpretation.

The distinction between legislative interpretation and judicial interpretation is made by the Standing Committee of the NPC: "Any law or statute which requires a further definition or supplementary rule is to be interpreted by the Standing Committee of the NPC";[129] any question which concerns the "substantial application of a law or statute in the judicial process is to be interpreted by the Judicial Committee of the Supreme People's Court."[130] That is to say, the judiciary only has power to interpret the ambiguities of law as applied to the judicial process. The Supreme People's Court has no right to make an interpretation in those cases which do not arise from the application of the law during the judicial process. In other words, the power of "judicial review" actually resides in the legislature, or the Standing Committee of the NPC, rather than in the Supreme Court. In the Chinese legal system, the *real* power of interpretation of the law is legislative and *not* judicial.

The people's procuratorate, in order to supervise the correct interpretation of law, has the power to prosecute any distorted interpretation of the law. However, since the National People's Congress is the highest organ of state authority and the Standing Committee its standing organ, the Supreme People's Procuratorate is responsible to them and reports to them. For this reason, the people's procuratorate cannot prosecute the interpretation of law by the NPC or its Standing Committee. In case the Chief Procurator of the Supreme People's Procuratorate disagrees with the interpretation of the Judicial Committee of the Supreme People's Court, he has authority to submit the case to the Standing Committee of the NPC for final review and disposition.

In the interpretation of law, Chinese jurists use the method of "grammatical analysis" to illustrate the meaning of words used in provisions. For example, Article 2 of the Marriage Law states: "... and the exaction of money or gifts in connection with marriage, shall be prohibited."[131] In application, the courts held that the meaning of this Article was not conclusive. Therefore, the Legal Commission of the former Central People's Government interpreted the law by saying that "the exaction of money or gift in connection with marriage means the open purchase of marriage or the disguised purchase of marriage. As to the willing help or grants given by parents or the male and female parties, this is not prohibited."[132] The Chinese Communists also interpret the law through the method of "expanded meaning". For

139

example, Article 4 of the Provisional Regulations Governing the Management of Foreign Trade states: "Any foreign businessman or foreign corporation that intends to carry on export and import business in our country and is willing to observe the laws and decrees of our country...may start business at an appointed location upon the completion of registration at the Foreign Trade Administration in that location."[133] Literally, there is a distinction between the words law (fa-lu) and statute (fa-ling) in China, and only those documents enacted by the Standing Committee of the NPC are called decrees. Yet, in this article, the word "decree" has been interpreted in a broader sense that it includes all laws, decrees, and governmental directives.

This broader interpretation of law should not be confused with the application of law by analogy. Expansive interpretation extends only the literal meaning of legal privisions, not the scope of application of a given law. It is not permissible to make application by analogy to a given case because of the conclusiveness of other legal rules. Whether a law can be applied by analogy is an issue which must be determined on the basis of the express rules of that law or the interpretation of the legislature. The authority that applies the law cannot decide the issue arbitrarily. It is normally decided by the organ which has the power of "legislative interpretation", namely, the NPC. Finally, the most important of all: To interpret law without taking the current political situation into consideration will result in the "danger of departing from reality", that is from politics.

The Character and
Function of
Criminal Law

After the establishment of the People's Republic, the Common Program, as a provisional constitution, was promulgated together with other laws and decrees which, by nature of criminal laws, were designed for the sole purpose of suppression of counter-revolutionaries. The laws[134] and the military tribunals concentrated their efforts to prevent any threat to overthrow the Communist regime.

In order to restrict and attack the "national bourgeoisie", the party and the government in 1952 organized the entire nation to launch the "Three-Anti" and "Five-Anti" movement. In the same year, the Central People's Government promulgated the "Anti-Corruption Act", imposing legal penalties not only on corruption, but also on many other criminal acts, i.e., stealing. Along this line, many criminal statutes, orders and resolutions were issued. For example, the Provisional Regulations on Punishment for Unlawful Landlords";[135] "Instruction of Suppression of Counter-Revolutionary Activities";[136] "Provisional Penal Act on Endangering State Currency";[137] "Provisional Act on Safeguarding State Secrets":[138] and the "Election Law of the National People's Congress and Local People's Congresses"[139] in which provisions were made concerning the criminal responsibility for obstructing elections. All these laws and statutory decrees played a vital role in maintaining the new government and social order in the first years of the People's Republic.

The promulgation of the 1954 Constitution marked the opening of a new era in the Chinese legal system. In the form of law, the Constitution laid down general principles for the transitional period of Communist China, explicitly regulated the ways and means to realize socialism, and provided China's political system as well as the people's rights and duties. All these provisions form the basis of criminal legislation of Communist China. Later, the government promulgated some criminal statutes, such as the "Apprehension and Detention Act."[140] For the first time under the Communist legal system, the criminal statute defines the criminal responsibility for unlawful arrest and detention.[141] Besides, in accordance with the resolution adopted on September 26, 1954 by the First Session of the First National People's Congress, "...all the existing laws and decrees enacted and approved by the Central People's Government since founding of the PRC on October 1, 1949 shall remain in force unless in conflict with the Constitution."[142] Some of those statutes and decrees were enacted by the NPC and its Standing Committee or the former Council of the Central People's Government; some were promulgated by the administrative organs, such as the State Council of the former GAC or regional councils of military and political affairs. Others were issued by the Supreme People's Court.

The primary function of the criminal law during the early period of the People's Republic was, as the communists rationalized, nothing more than "to emancipate the people from the reactionary rule and to establish the revolutionary order".[143] Thus, all statutes and decrees were simple and general rather than comprehensive and codified. After China entered the period of planned economic programs, the change in the political and economic conditions of the state required a corresponding improvement in the legal system. The 1954 Constitution further unified legislative power. That is to say, the NPC is the only organ that exercises the law-making power of the state.[144] The NPC and its Standing Committee gradually became the principle sources of criminal law.

142

Since law is a part of the superstructure built on the economic foundation, it reflects the economic condition of society, which in turn determines the character and nature of law. The Chinese Communists pointed out that it is an illusion for the jurists to believe that society is based on law. Rather, law is based on society because it reflects the common interest and needs produced by the mode of material production in society.[145] In short, the nature of law, which expresses the will of the ruling class, is determined by the nature of the economic foundation of the society. Since the development of the social productive forces and promotion of the individual material life will have to rely on the economic foundation built on the socialist system of ownership, the slogan, "everything for socialism", has become the guidance of everything in China.

Without exception, the criminal law serves an effective instrument of party policies. It regards that behavior which endangers the people's democratic system and socialist order as a crime. To sum up, the criminal law of Communist China has the following characteristics: (1) It is not inherited from the Kuomintang's law system and deals primarily with "the enemies of socialism"; (2) Most of the criminal statutes and decrees are first drafted by the Party through investigation and experimentation; (3) The nature of the punishments emphasized is on education and reform rather than "retaliationalism and penalism"; (4) The criminal law of Communist China has its political role in educating the masses "socialistically and communistically".

The retroactivity of the criminal law. The principle of Chinese Communist law prohibits retroactivity of criminal law. But in certain special cases, the criminal law of Communist China can be applied retroactively to acts committed after the establishment of the Communist regime which have

143

not been tried or still are pending.[146] Serious
"criminal" acts committed before the Communist
government came into existence are also punishable by the people's courts.[147]

Some statutes, for example, the Counter-Revolutionary Act,[148] have explicitly provided for
retroactivity. Most of them do not have similar
provisions, but communist jurists maintain that
their retroactivity is expressed clearly in the
legislative reports. For example, the Anti-Corruption Act[149] does not expressly provide that it
is retroactive, but the legislative report indicates that the Act can be applied retroactive to
those who violated its provisions before it came
into force.[150] However, in corruption and theft
cases where the degree of offense is serious or
popular resentment is high, then, the time limits
of prosecution may be counted back to the days
before the Communist control of Chinese Mainland.

Some other criminal statutes neither expressly provide for retroactivity, nor do they have
legislative reports explaining their retroactivity, such as the "Provisional Statute on Penalties for Undermining the State Monetary System".[151]
This statute has been interpreted as a retroactive law against those offenses undermining
national currency before its promulgation. The
legal interpretation simply justified that "every
citizen knows that forgery or alteration of national currency is illegal even before the promulgation of this Act."[152] Furthermore, the provisional constitution provided: "Whoever engages
oneself in monetary speculation or destroys the
State's monetary enterprise shall be severely
punished."[153] It provides legal ground for the
people's courts to punish those who committed offenses prior to the enactment of the Act.

The western concept against retroactivity of
criminal laws, and the attitude that it is unjust
to convict a person for an act which was legal
when it was done, have little place in the criminal law of Communist China.

To sum up, the Chinese Communist criminal statutes can be applied retroactively to all those offenses that have not been tried or are still pending judgment. In other words, to all these offenses, the new law shall be applied. But if the penalty of the old law or statutory decree is lighter than the penalty of the new law, the old law or statutory decree should be applied.[154]

Crime by analogy. In Chinese Communist criminal law, analogy is the application of the most similar provisions in the existing criminal legislation to convict and punish "socially dangerous acts"[155] which are not expressly provided for by the criminal statutes as offenses. Analogy is an inevitable necessity when the written criminal statutes are still in the process of codification. According to the principles of criminal law, a doer is held to be criminally responsible for his act only when this act violates the law and deserves punishment. This is known as the principle of *nullum crimen sine lege*. However, if the doer's act is "socially dangerous in substance and deserves punishment,"[156] though not expressly provided for by any criminal statute, the criminal law of Communist China, by analogy, would apply "the most similar provisions in the existing criminal statutes to convict and punish the doer."[157]

The application of analogy in the Chinese Communist criminal law is closely related with the current political and economic situation. At present, the People's Republic is in the stage of transition from political consolidation and economic reconstruction through socialism toward complete communism. Thus, "everything is in a state of constant development and change, and the offenses committed by the criminals are various in type."[158] The situation, accordingly, could not have been accurately estimated and comprehensively covered by the legislators when they enacted the criminal laws. The existing criminal statutes cannot possibly include all the provisions for

every single crime which may appear. Thus, it
is necessary to allow the courts and judges to
hear cases and to pass judgments by analogy.
For that reason, the Counter-Revolutionary Act
expressly provides for the use of analogy.[159]

The Chinese Communists realized the weakness
and unfairness in the application of analogy and
declared that after several years when the state
socialist construction develops further, and the
criminal law becomes more complete, they "may consider to abolish the system of analogy."[160]
Under the present circumstances, however, they
explained that the political and economic conditions allow no alternative but to apply the
method of analogy.

In Chinese Communist criminal law, to determine an offense is regarded as an important "political task" of the court and the procuratorate.
It is necessary for them to make serious analysis
of the doer's act to determine whether or not it
constitutes an offense.

Before the codification of Chinese criminal
law, the clear and present evidence upon which an
offense is established is determined by individual criminal statutes, such as the Counter-Revolutionary Act, the Anti-Corruption Act, or by
judges, procurators, or public security officers
according to party and government policies, statutory decrees, instructions, and even by their
personal experience and knowledge without relying
on the principle of "no crime without a law".

Punishment. In the criminal law of Communist
China, punishment is "a coercive means employed
by the people's court to protect the interests of
the state and people,"[161] and a form of "class
struggle". It is a "sharp weapon" used by the
state authorities "to eliminate the enemies and
the antagonistic elements".[162] However, the relationship between punishment and harm in Communist China is ambiguous. The concept that punishment is to be inflicted in proportion to the

146

gravity of the harm has often been disregarded. That is to say, the concept that the severity of punishment should be balanced with the harmfulness of the offense has been discarded, and that ethical significance in harm and punishment has also been ignored in the criminal law of Communist China. For example, in a factory where production was high, labor efficiently managed, and the accident rate low, a worker who negligently violated a regulation and thereby caused an accident fatal to another worker was convicted in a mass trial presided over by a people's judge and was given a suspended sentence of two years. In a similar factory where the production rate was low and the accident rate high, a worker who committed the same type of "crime" was charged as a counter-revolutionary element and sentenced to life imprisonment.[163] What made the punishments in the two cases different was presumably not the gravity of the harms done, nor was it the nature of the act committed. This unequal punishment for equal offenses is understandable as a reflection of a policy which requires a severe and deterrent punishment in a factory with a low rate of production and high percentage of accident "to suppress the bad elements and to deter the potential criminals in that area".[164]

The explicitly declared objectives of punishment in the criminal law of Communist China are: (1) suppression and deterrence, (2) education, and (3) reformation.[165] Deterrence as an objective of the criminal punishment has always been emphasized in the Communist law. "Punishment serves a warning to all unstable elements in society."[166] and "to deny the role of our punishment in deterring the enemies is unrealistic and, therefore, erroneous."[167] In the suppression of counter-revolutionaries, deterrence has been espoused as the most salient and powerful aspect of criminal punishment. Public execution of various punishments, e.g., reprimand, public humiliation, and the death penalty, was commonly used by the people's

tribunals in mass trials.[168] Suppression is directed to "the class enemies of socialism", while
education and reformation are used in coping with
so-called "contradictions among the people".

   Reprimand. It is often called *Pea-ping Chiao-
yu* or "criticism-education", and sometimes "admonition", "reproof", or "an order to apologize". It
is the lightest punishment applied by the people's
court — mostly to petty offenses.[169] The method
of "criticism-education" is diversified. Sometimes
it takes place in the court and is sermonized by
the people's judge, and sometimes the convicted
person is ordered to put a public notice in a newspaper expressing his apology and repentance for
the offense which he has committed, or to parade
along the streets with a sign on his back describing his evil behavior.[170] Perhaps it is more
noteworthy that in some cases the convicted are
ordered by the court to pay monetary compensation
to the victims.[171] However, it is by no means
clear who the offender is supposed to compensate
in cases where the crime is not one that damaged
individual or property, as, for example, in the
criminal offense of spreading rumors.[172] Equally
significant is the fact that punishment by reprimand is applied by the people's court in civil
disputes as well as in criminal cases.[173] There
are no definite rules of procedure in these cases.

   Surveillance. It is "a punishment whereby
the punished is subject to labor reform under
the control of state organs and under mass supervision."[174] In the earlier years of the Communist
regime, surveillance was primarily employed to
those counter-revolutionaries whose offenses were
relatively insignificant but were punishable by
less severe penalties than imprisonment. For example, Article 3 of the Anti-Corruption Act provided that surveillance is applicable to those
"who may not be imprisoned but shall be deprived
of political rights, partially or wholly, for a
given period of time and shall be reformed through

labor.[175] Later, under the criminal law of Communist China, surveillance was also applied as a punishment to those who were dangerous to social order, such as thieves, gamblers, and racketeers.[176] Thus, "surveillance", which is, in substance, the same as "supervised labor" is sometimes confused with the administrative sanction, but is deemed to be a different and more severe sanction because it is imposed by a court for the commission of crime.[177]

Since 1956, the Standing Committee of the National People's Congress issued a decision which provided that the surveillance of counter-revolutionaries and other criminals should be decided by the people's court and executed by the public security organ.[178] Hence, it becomes clear that "surveillance" is applicable to both counter-revolutionaries and other criminal cases and must be decided by the people's court. In certain regions, for example, the border areas, where there are an insufficient number of the people's courts, the authority for "surveillance" is exercised by the nonjudicial or extra-legal organs, namely the party organs. Most of the cases involving the surveillance of counter-revolutionaries are directly determined and enforced by public security bureaus. The purpose for placing petty offenders under "mass control" or "mass surveillance" is that they can transform themselves into new persons[179] under the observation of the government and surveillance of the masses by means of ideological education.[180] Since 1956, the power to put a person under surveillance can only be exercised by a people's court, but public security members still have influence in these cases. For instance, while the maximum term of control is officially three years,[181] it may be extended beyond or reduced at the discretion of the public security officer or the "mass" represented by local Party members.[182]

In Communist China, criminal sanctions are employed for the deterrence and suppression of "reactionary elements", while reform through labor and criticism-education is used for rehabilitation of the "people" prior to the imposition of severe punishment.[183]   Public execution of the death penalty[184] and of various punishments, e.g., imprisonment,[185] is widely used to achieve these objectives.

Chinese Communists have been criticized by the Russians for their failure to codify law, and for their divergence from socialist legal theory.[186] However, formal codification of criminal law could hardly be a solution to the problems existing in the legal system of Communist China, because law is subordinated to party policies. It is necessary for the Communist leaders that the certainty and regularity of the law yield to the need for elasticity and flexibility. One can hardly avoid the conclusion that the legal system of Communist China, under the influence of Maoist-Leninist-Marxist ideology, is one in which order is superior to justice, and the law, particularly the criminal law, is largely a political codification of the party policies.

NOTES

1.   See Article 17, *The Common Programme of the Chinese People's Political Consultative Conference,* September 27, 1949. It served as the provisional constitution until the promulgation of the 1954 Constitution. Hereinafter cited as *The Common Programme.*

2.   Andre Bonnichon, "Law in Communist China," *Journal of International Commission of Jurists* (Winter 1955), p. 4.

3.   Article 17, *supra,* note 1.

4.   Felix Greene, *Awakened China* (Garden City, N.Y.: Doubleday, 1961), p. 191.

5.   Bonnichon, *op.cit.*, p. 3.

6.   Liang Shih, "The Judicial System in New China," *People's China*, No. 12 (June 16, 1957), p. 15.

7.   *People's Daily*, (September 15, 1957).

8.   Pi-wu Tung, "Report on the Work of the Supreme People's Court," *Current Background* (September 19, 1956).

9.   Pi-wu Tung, "Judicial Work in China in the Past Year," *Current Background* (July 3, 1956).

10.   *Ibid.*

11.   Te-feng Wu, "To Defend the Socialist Legal System" (Broadcast speech made at the Central People's Broadcasting Station on January 19, 1958) *Political-Legal Research*, No. 1 (1958), p. 10.

12.   Kuang-teh Yang, "Going to Law in Peking," *China Reconstructs*, No. 5 (1956). p. 18.

13.   Liang Shih, *op.cit.*, p. 18.

14.   See "Recent Legal Developments in the People's Republic of China," *Bulletin of the International Commission of Jurists*, No. 8, (December 1958), p. 7.

15.   Paul Duez and Guy Debeyre, *Traite de droit administratif* (Paris: 1952), p. 203.

16.   *Ibid.*, p. 205.

17.   *Ibid.*, p. 207.

18.   Such as prohibition of the export of rice; prohibitions of the raising of rice prices; of the

increasing of rent; of the revocation of the lease of land; and of gambling and opium, etc.

19. See *The Peasant Movement in the Period of the First Revolutionary Civil War* (Peking: People's Press, 1953), p. 356.

20. Actually it was a Party's order, the "Instruction on the Abolition of the Kuomintang's Six Codes and the Establishment of the Judicial Principles in Liberated Areas".

21. Ch'ing Chao, "Several Problems Concerning Law and Policy", *Science of Law*, No. 2 (1958), p. 23.

22. Wu Ta-ying, "The Nature and Characteristics of Socialist Law," *Science of Law*, No. 3 (1958), p. 27.

23. Chia-chu Chien, "The Social and Economic System During the Transitional Period of Our Country", *Political-Legal Research*, No. 3 (1955).

24. Article 1 of the *Constitution*.

25. Article 5 of the *Constitution*.

26. Ta-ying Wu, *op.cit.*, p. 26.

27. *Ibid.*

28. *Principles of Marxism and Leninism* (Peking: People's Press, 1959), p. 794.

29. Pi-wu Tung, "Judicial Work in China in the Past Year," *Current Background*, July 3, 1956; p. 24.

30.   B. Meissner, *The Legal Position of the Communist Party of the Soviet Union* (Chinese translation, Peking: People's Press, 1962), p. 23.

31.   *New Justice* (Munich, 1954), p. 97.

32.   *Ibid.*, p. 67.

33.   See I-tai Keng, "Protecting the Party's Leadership in the People's Courts; Refuting the Absurd Contention of Trial Independence", *Cheng-fa Chiao-hsueh (Political-Legal Teachings)* No. 1 (1958), p. 15.

34.   See Article 59, Chapter IX, *The Constitution of the Communist Party of China,* adopted by the Eighth National Congress of the Communist Party of China, September 26, 1956.   English text can be found in Blaustein, *Fundamental Legal Documents of Communist China* (South Hackensack, New Jersey: Fred B. Rothman & Co., 1962) pp. 55-95.   Hereinafter cited as *The Constitution of CPC*.

35.   See Articles 43, 44, 45, and 46 of *The Constitution of CPC*.

36.   Chang Hao, "The Position and Function of Socialist Laws in People's Democratic Dictatorship", *Political-Legal Research,* No. 4 (1962), p. 26.

37.   *Ibid.,* p. 28.

38.   N. V. Krylenko, "Structure of Courts in the USSR", quoted by Strogovich in *Handbook of Soviet Criminal Procedure* (Moscow, 1960), p. 76.

39.   Section 3 of the *Soviet Principles of the Law on the Judiciary* (December 25, 1958).

40.   *Organic Law of the People's Courts,* 1954.

41. *Ibid.*, Article 3.

42. *The Constitution of Communist China* provides that the National People's Congress (NPC) is the highest organ of state authority in the People's Republic (Article 21), and the only legislative authority in the country (Article 22).

43. The State Council has substantial executive powers. Many major policies were decided, at least formally, by the State Council. As Prof. George Yu regards that "it is the most important instrument in implementing the policies of the Party." See *Government of Communist China,* ed. by Yu (San Francisco: Chandler, 1966), p. 253. According to Article 49 (2) of the Constitution, the State Council exercises the function and power "to submit proposals on laws and other matters to the National People's Congress or its Standing Committee".

44. *People's Daily* (March 23, 1962).

45. "Report on Chinese Law" by the editor of *Cheng-fa Yen-Chiu* in *Political-Legal Research* No. 3, (1962), pp. 23-24.

46. *Ibid.*

47. Included in the Chinese socialist legal system are the branches of state law, civil law, criminal law, administration law, financial law, labor law, agricultural cooperative law, marriage law, law governing judicial proceedings, etc. Each' of these branches of law reflects certain social relations, and in turn, governs these social relations. The distinction between these branches of law which govern different social relations is determined by the nature of the different social relations.

154

48. Regarding the nature of property relations, opinions vary in the contemporary world of law. Some hold that it is a kind of ideological social relation; others maintain that it is a sort of material social relation, namely, an economic relation. The Chinese Communists consider that the latter is more correct and exact. See "Discussion on the Governing Objective of the Civil Law," *People's Daily* (Jan. 16, 1957).

49. Property relations other than these are regulated by other branches of law. For example, property relations arising from activities in financial administration and administrative management, such as tax collection, budgetary appropriation, allocation of funds, etc., are regulated by the financial law and administrative law. Property relations in connection with labor relations, such as wages, allowances, welfare, etc., are regulated by the labor law.

50. *People's Daily*, (January 16, 1957).

51. *Ibid.*

52. *Ibid.*

53. *Ibid.*

54. *Ibid.*

55. Pi-wu Tung, "Judicial Work in China in the Past Year", p. 15.

56. *Ibid.*, p. 17

57. Article 1, Section I, *The Agrarian Reform Law of the People's Republic of China,* 1950.

58. *Ibid.*, Article 10, 11, 12; Section III.

59. See Article 30, Section V.

60.   See *Labor Capital Consultative Councils in Private Enterprises,* a directive issued by the Ministry of Labor, 1950.

61.   *Ibid.*

62.   For an excellent treatment on the Constitution, see Franklin W. Houn, "Communist China's New Constitution", *The Western Political Quarterly,* June, 1955, cf. H. Arthur Steiner, "Constitutionalism in Communist China", *The American Political Science Review,* (March, 1955), pp. 1-21.

63.   Article 4, *The Agrarian Reform Law.*

64.   *Ibid.*

65.   *Chang Chiang Jih Pao (Chang Chiang Daily),* September 6, 1954.

66.   *Ibid.*

67.   *Decision of the State Council on Certain Matters In The Current Socialist Transformation of Private Industry, Commerce and Handicraft Industry; Regulations of the State Council Governing the Practice of Fixed Interest in State-Private Joint Enterprises; Regulations of the State Council Governing the Main Issues on Property Liquidation and Estimation of Private Enterprises before the Practice of State-Private Joint Operation,* all issued on 8 February 1956.

68.   *Basic Problems in the Civil Law of the People's Republic of China,* Peking, 1958, The Central Political-Judicial Cadres' School; translated by U. S. Joint Publications Research Service, 1961.

69.   Chou En-lai, "Political Report to the 8th National Congress of the Communist Party of China", September 1956.

70. See Articles 4, 5, 6, of the *Constitution*.

71. Article 6 of the *Constitution*.

72. See Preamble of the *Constitution*.

73. Article 10 of the *Constitution*.

74. Article 15 of the *Constitution*.

75. The information is based primarily on an interview with Mr. Miao Ron Chang, a Shanghai industrialist who abandoned his business and left the Chinese Mainland in 1962. Mr. Chang and his family now live in Montreal, Canada.

76. Article 85 of the *Constitution*.

77. Article 86 of the *Constitution*.

78. Shao-chi Liu, "Report on the Draft Constitution of the People's Republic of China", delivered at the First Session of the First National People's Congress on September 15, 1954, pp. 38-39.

79. *Basic Problems in the Civil Law*, p. 32.

80. *Ibid*.

81. Shao-chi Liu, *supra*, note 78, p. 39.

82. Article 14 of the *Constitution*.

83. *Basic Problems in the Civil Law*, pp. 164-168.

84. *Ibid*., pp. 342-352.

85. The others are the Agrarian Law and the Trade Union Law, all of which were enacted in 1950.

86. "The biggest popular movement that has so far taken place in 1953 was a tremendous educational campaign to publicize the Marriage Law and to endorse it." See Yen Fang, "Making the Marriage Law Work", *China Reconstructs*, Vol. 5, (1953), p. 31.

87. See Chih-jang Chang, (then Vice-President of the Supreme People's Court), "A much Needed Marriage Law", *People's Daily* (April 17, 1950).

88. See S. L. Fu, "The New Marriage Law of People's Republic of China", *Contemporary China* (Hong Kong University Press), Vol. I (1955), p. 122.

89. Quoted *ibid*.

90. Article 1, *The Marriage Law of the People's Republic of China*. Hereinafter cited as *The Marriage Law*.

91. Article 2, *The Marriage Law*.

92. Chih-jang Chang, *op.cit*.

93. Article 6, *The Marriage Law*.

94. Comment was made during the preliminary discussion with the author on the dissertation outline in August 1966.

95. Article 9, *The Marriage Law*.

96. Article 26, *ibid*.

97. See Vermier Y. Chiu, "Marriage Laws of the Ch'ing Dynasty, the Republic of China and Communist China", *Contemporary China*, Vol. II, 1956-1957, p. 72; and Ch'ing-kun Yang, *The Chinese Family in the Communist Revolution* (Cambridge, Mass.: MIT Press, 1959).

98. E. g., Government Administration Council, State Council.

99. Up to date, Communist China has no formal codified law. The directives and regulations of the administrative agencies are regarded as laws.

100. *Basic Problems in the Civil Law*, p. 37.

101. *Ibid.*, p. 38.

102. *Basic Problems in the Civil Law*, p. 37.

103. *Ibid.*, p. 38.

104. *Ibid.*, p. 39.

105. "The Third National Conference on Judiciary Work", *Hsin-hua Pan-yueh Kan* (New China Biweekly), No. 83 (May 1956).

106. *Ibid.*

107. *Ibid.*

108. Promulgated in May, 1954. For text see *FKHP*, Vol. 2, 1954.

109. Promulgated by the Central People's Government, June 30, 1950.

110. Article 1, *Agrarian Reform Law*.

111. See Section 1, Article 60 of the *Constitution*.

112. Section 4, Article 70 of the *Constitution*.

113. Article 27, Chapter VIII, *The Marriage Law*.

114. *Basic Problems in the Civil Law*, p. 43.

115. *Ibid.*, p. 44.

116. Communist China emphasized, as well as all other nations, the equality of the law. However, it is interesting to note here that the civil law has "absolute power of command over the citizen" indicated law and Party policy are two in one.

117. A juridical person, under the Chinese civil law, means a social entity participating in civil activities, such as a private corporation and a state enterprise are all juristic persons under the civil law.

118. E.g., *The Marriage Law*.

119. E.g., *The Provisional Regulations Governing the Liquidation and Estimation of the State Enterprise Capital*, promulgated by the Commission on Financial and Economic Affairs of the former Council of State Affairs in July 1951.

120. Article 2, Section 2, *The Provisional Regulations Governing Special Treatment of Foreign Diplomats and Consuls*.

121. *Ibid.*

122. *Ibid.*

123. *Ibid.*

124. Such as the Government Administration Council, Council of the State Affairs.

125. See Chapter VI.

126. *Ibid.*

127.   Shih-Chieh Chou, "A Preliminary Study of Legal Relationship in Civil Procedure", *Chiao-hsueh Chien-pao* (Teaching Bulletin), No. 26 (June 1957), p. 29.

128.   In fact, an official legislative interpretation of law is equivalent to the Judicial Review of the Supreme Court in the United States.

129.   "Resolution on the Question of Legal Interpretation" adopted by the Standing Committee of the NPC in its 17th Session on June 23, 1955.

130.   *Ibid.*

131.   *The Marriage Law.*

132.   "Interpretation of Certain Questions in the Enforcement of the Marriage Law", quoted in *Basic Problems in the Civil Law,* p. 52.

133.   See *FKHP,* Vol. 5.

134.   E.g., *Counter-Revolutionary Act of the People's Republic of China* of 1951.

135.   Enacted by Regional Administration, November 1950.

136.   Issued jointly by the GAC (Government Administration Council) and the Supreme People's Court in July 1950.

137.   By GAC in April 1951.

138.   By GAC in June 1951.

139.   Promulgated by the Central People's Government on March 1, 1953.

140.   December 20, 1954.   *FKHP,* Vol. I, p. 239.

141. See Article 12, *Apprehension and Detention Act.*

142. *FKHP*, Vol. I. p. 104.

143. Shao-chi Liu, *Political Report of the Central Committee of the Communist Party of China to the Eighth National Congress of the Party.* September 1956.

144. Article 22 of the *Constitution.*

145. See *Complete Writings of Marx and Engels,* Russian ed., Vol. 7, p. 254. Quoted in Vyshinsky, *On the Question of the Theory of State and Law.* (Peking: Legal Press, 1955), p. 202.

146. *Principles of Criminal Law,* p. 32.

147. According to Article 18, *Counter-Revolutionary Act*: "This Statute is also applicable to counter-revolutionary crimes committed before it came into effect."

148. Article 18.

149. The term "corruption" in Chinese law is a legal term carrying the meaning of embezzlement, bribery, stealing public property, etc. The *Anti-Corruption Act* has detailed descriptions.

150. "Report on the Drafting of the Anti-Corruption Act of the People's Republic of China," April 1952.

151. Adopted by the State Administrative Council, April 19, 1951. English text can be found in Blaustein, *op. cit.,* pp. 233-236.

152. *Principles of Criminal Law,* p. 33.

153. Article 39, *The Common Programme*.

154. *Principles of Criminal Law*, p. 36.

155. Chinese Communists use the term "act" *(Hsin-wei)* to designate human conduct that is relevant in the penal law.

156. *Principles of Criminal Law*, p. 54

157. *Ibid.*

158. *Ibid.*

159. Article 16 of the Act provides: "Persons who have committed other crimes for counter-revolutionary purposes that are not specified in that Statute are subject to the punishment applicable to the crimes which most closely resemble those specified in these Statutes."

160. *Principles of Criminal Law*, p. 55.

161. *Ibid.*, p. 147.

162. The persistent use of law as a measure of suppression in China has been severely criticized by the Soviet Union. See John N. Hazard, "Unity and Diversity in Socialist Law", *Law and Contemporary Problems*, Vol. 30 (1965), p. 270. For example, in February, 1970, more than 40 persons were executed in Canton for their criminal acts of food robbery, arson, sabotage, and "destroy the national economy." *Central Daily News* (March 27, 1970), p. 1.

163. The source of the case was originally collected from the refugees from mainland China.

164. It is not merely a political slogan but a political policy of the CPC. See Lo Jui-ching,

"Report to the Third Session of the First National People's Congress" in *People's Daily* (June 24, 1956).

165.   *Principles of Criminal Law*, pp. 148-151.

166.   *Ibid.*, p. 150.

167.   *Ibid.*

168.   Dorothy Thompson, "The People's Tribunals: The Anti-thesis of Justice", *American Bar Association Journal*, Vol. 40 (1954), p. 289.   For example, 24 persons were sentenced to death by the People's Tribunal of Canton in a mass trial on February 20, 1970.   *Central Daily News* (March 27, 1970), p. 1.

169.   *Principles of Criminal Law*, p. 162.

170.   This was exactly the same pattern of *Hsing-fa* (criminal punishment) that occurred in the time of Imperial China in the manner of public humiliation.

171.   *Ibid.*

172.   Article 10 (3) of the *Counter-Revolutionary Act*.

173.   *Principles of Criminal Law*, p. 163.

174.   *Ibid.*

175.   See P'eng Chen's "Report on the Drafting Anti-Corruption Act of the People's Republic of China", April 1952.

176.   Article 11 of the *Temporary Regulations for the Surveillance of Counter-Revolutionary Elements* authorized the power to the public security organs at the county or city level.   Adopted by

the State Administrative Council, June 27, 1952.
English text can be found in Blaustein, *op. cit.*,
pp. 222-226.   Hereinafter cited as *Surveillance
Regulations.*

177.   Article 12, *Surveillance Regulations.*

178.   "Decision of the Standing Committee of
the National People's Congress of the People's
Republic of China Relating to Control of Counter-
Revolutionary Elements Uniformly by Judgement of
a People's Court", November 17, 1956.   Text can
be found in *FKHP,* Vol. 4, p. 246.

179.   *Principles of Criminal Law,* p. 164.

180.   Article 2, *Surveillance Regulations.*

181.   Article 6, *Surveillance Regulations.*

182.   During the period of surveillance, if
the person has shown good attitude, really felt
sorry for what he has done in the past, or has
established merits, the responsible executing
organ may request the court to reduce his term
of surveillance.   On the other hand, the person
equally can be requested to extend his term if
he misbehaves himself during the surveillance.
For the influence of the police and security agencies in criminal cases, see *Principles of Criminal Law,* p. 167; cf. Cohen, *The Communism of
Mao Tse-tung* (Chicago: The University of
Chicago Press, 1964), p. 522.

183.   For the differentiation between *peo-
ple* and *enemy* under the People's Republic, see
O. Edmund Clubb, *Twentieth Century China* (New
York: Columbia University Press, 1964), Chap.
9.   Cf. Mao Tse-tung, "On People's Democratic
Dictatorship."

184. *Principles of Criminal Law*, pp. 172-176.

185. *Ibid.*, pp. 169-172.

186. See Hazard, "Unity and Diversity in Socialist Law", *op. cit.*

6   Legal Institutions of the People's Republic

Justice is an essential element of law, but law is not the equivalent of justice. They are inter-related but by no means identical. Within the framework of Chinese Communist legality, justice is mostly administered without formal court trials; and the role of the judiciary is secondary to that of administrative authorities. Underlying this phenomenon is the Marxist notion that judicial functions must be gradually transferred to social organizations, so that society can function by itself in the future without the state. Thus, a dual system has been established whereby adminis-trative sanctions are applied to ordinary offenses and legal penalties are prepared for crimes con-sidered highly dangerous to the state.

As a consequence, the state's legal system op-erates through two parallel channels. First, there is the constitutional judicial hierarchy consist-ing of the Supreme People's Court in Peking, high courts in provinces, intermediate courts in spec-ial districts, and lower courts in *hsien* (counties).

Political control over this court system is assured by two devices: party organizations function in the courts at all levels and influence judicial decisions by virtue of the procuratorates' right to protest objectionable judgments. There is no institutional foundation for an independent judiciary.[1]

Secondly, paralleling the courts, there is a host of institutions exercising quasi-judicial and disciplinary powers, such as comrades adjudication committees,[2] people's mediation (or conciliation) committees, and party organized mass (assembly) meetings. The main functions of these extra-legal or quasi-judicial bodies are to settle civil disputes among individuals and to punish those who commit minor offenses or violate socialist discipline. In his 1957 "Rectification Movement Report", Party Secretary Teng Hsiao-p'ing made it clear that political opponents are subject to criminal punishment, while those who "never commit major crimes but often commit petty offenses" are to be disciplined by social institutions in order to reduce the burden of the courts. In short, legal institutions in Communist China function primarily for two purposes: to punish the enemies of the state and to secure stability for the development of the national economy.

The basic means of social control under the communist government is not law, but the police or the public security force. Police control applies to the population in general, and breaches of law are subject to two basic types of punishment: administrative sanction, mainly by labor reform, and the legal, i.e., by decisions of the courts. Official statistics show that up to 1956 there were only about 2,100 practicing lawyers (paid by the State), 670 legal counselling offices to serve 1,972 counties (hsien) and 171 cities.[3] There were 3,000 Basic Courts, 200 Intermediate Courts, and 28 Higher Courts.[4]

The Organization of
the Judiciary

A number of articles in the Common Programme determined the basic tasks of the people's courts
in relation to the suppression of counter-revolution,[5] land reform, [6] strenghtening of the state
machinery of the People's Republic,[7] etc. Prior
to the adoption of the 1954 Constitution, the
Common Programme has been the basic document governing the activity of the people's courts.
    The composition of the Supreme Court was rat-
ified by the first session of the Central People's
Government Council, and it immediately assumed
its functions. At the same time, the Judicial
Commission of the Central Committee of the Party
continued its preparation of an All-Chinese law
based on the Soviet legal system.[8] In northern
China, 384 people's courts were established, 362
in eastern China, and 340 in south-central part
of China.[9] The function of suppressing counter-
revolutionary elements was taken over by the courts
and the institutions of public security. By the
fall of 1951, the Central People's Government
Council adopted the Provisional Regulations Governing the Organization of the People's Courts.[10]
    It must be noted that the percentage of Kuo-
mintang judicial workers in the Communist court
system was quite high. Prior to the "Judicial
Reform", nearly 6,000, or about 22 percent, of the
judges were staff of the preceeding government.
In the city court of Shanghai, for instance, out
of a total of 104 judges, 80 were members of the
Kuomintang judicial system. In the cities of
Wuhan and Canton and the provinces of Kwangtung,
Kiangsi, and Kwangsi, the number of former judicial staff reached a total of 64 percent.[11]
    In August 1952, the Communist Party of China
called on the nation for a mass movement for judicial reform. The reform was carried out in two
basic directions: (1) the direction of ridding
court staff of reactionary elements among the

workers of the old judicial system and also new workers under the influence of former Kuomintang court officials; (2) the direction of eradication of the old legal concepts and methods.[12]

During the process of judicial reform, with wide participation of the masses, all administrative court staffs were overhauled from top to bottom, regardless of their original affiliations. All politically and morally "corrupted" personnel were removed from their offices. The replacement of these judges and court clerks was carried out on the basis of the following principles: (1) the core of the people's courts had to be composed of politically reliable personnel from among the workers of people's justice, who have been actively engaged in the mass movements "Sanfan"[13] and "Wufan";[14] (2) to supplement the staff of people's courts, those who have served in the people's tribunal should be selected with priority.[15]

The second direction of the judicial reform — the revision of the style of judicial work and the ideological concept of law — was rather a complicated one. It was not only necessary to re-educate the "legal conscience" of the court personnel, but also to overcome the traditional concepts of the masses about law and courts. The Minister of Justice expressed that "it is not enough to limit ourselves only to the problem of the personnel inside the courts, it is also necessary to eradicate the remnants of the Kuomintang law in our ideology .... It is, therefore, necessary to mobilize the masses,...to conduct systematic propaganda of the precepts of Marxism-Leninism and the works of Mao Tse-tung on government and law...only in this way will it be possible to convert the courts into truly powerful instruments of the democratic dictatorship of the people."[16]

On September 10, 1953, Premier Chou En-lai signed an order on carrying out the directive of the Ministry of Justice regarding the resolution adopted by the Second All-Chinese Conference of Judicial Workers. The order obligated the corresponding organs of the local people's governments to execute without deviation the terms of the resolution — the expansion of legal education throughout the country, and the necessity for the study of Marxism-Leninism and advanced Soviet experience of law.

Both the Constitution and the Organic Law of the People's Court of 1954 introduced some substantial changes in the organization of judiciary.

The Courts

The courts established by the Constitution were divided into Local People's Courts, Special People's Courts, and the Supreme Court. The Local People's Courts were subdivided into Basic People's Courts, Intermediate People's Courts, and Higher People's Courts.[17] The primary addition to this system since 1951 is the inclusion of Intermediate Courts.[18] The Presidents of all the courts are "elected" by the respective people's congresses at the corresponding levels.[19] The remaining judges, clerks are appointed by the local people's councils.[20]

The lower people's courts are the basic courts of first instance, i.e., in the absence of other provisions in the law, they try, in the first instance, both criminal and civil cases.[21] The Basic Court may petition the upper court to take jurisdiction of the trial if the case is sufficiently important.[22] The Basic Courts are granted the power to set up people's tribunals. The decisions of the people's tribunals are the decisions of the Basic Courts. Basic Courts are county and municipal courts, and each one is composed of a president, one or two vice-president, and several judges.[23]

The Basic Courts are the legal institutions which maintain the closest contact with the masses.

These courts also provide legal assistance, the public counselling offices which combined the former information bureaus, for preparing petitions and to aid illiterates. In the summer of 1954, the data concerning 22 provinces, ten large cities and the autonomous province of Inner Mongolia, there were more than 1,200 counselling offices in operation.[24] Their duties are: "To interpret questions relating to legal process and the law; to prepare petitions; to record verbal complaints and settle simple cases, which acquire no preliminary investigation or inquiries."[25] The examination of simple cases, in the simultaneous appearance of the petitioner and respondent, is preceeded by an attempt at reconciliation of the litigants; such attempts are also made when claims are presented in more complicated cases. In many instances, the litigants, after receiving appropriate explanations at the counselling office, refrain from litigation.

People's Conciliation Commissions. A unique institution of the Chinese Communist judicial system is the Conciliation Commission. It conducts, under the supervision of the Basic Courts but not in judicial form, hearings of civil disputes and minor criminal cases. It partakes some of the characteristics of the informal settlement of inter-family disputes traditionally undertaken by the elders on the village level. The Commissions were experimented with in the Shensi-Kansu-Ninghsia border region long before the establishment of the People's Republic, and was organized under the Provisional Organic Act of the People's Conciliation Commissions promulgated by the State Administrative Council on March 22, 1954.[26] The Commission operates, under the supervision of the courts of the first instance, on the village level in the countryside and on the precinct level in the cities.[27] They have a staff of three to eleven elected for one year terms by representatives of the population on the basis of correct politi-

cal thinking, impartial reputation, organizational ability, and enthusiasm for conciliatory work.[28]
The Commission functions within the framework of
government policy and law, acquires jurisdiction
through the consent of the disputants, and is forbidden to apply punishment or make arrests. It
should be noted that recourse to conciliation is
not a precondition to court litigation, and no
compulsion is admissable.[29] Concluded reconcil-
iations are registered by the Commission, and a
certificate issued to the litigants.[30] But
Courts have the right to amend or annul reconcil-
iations concluded by the Commission when they are
not in conformity with the policy of the government or its legislation.

The use of non-court Commissions to settle
minor disputes is certainly both in accord with
the Chinese tradition and in the interest of re-
lieving the burden of the courts. It also fulfills the function of legal education. The prevalent use of Conciliation Commissions may be seen
from the figure that, according to an imcomplete
survey for the province of Szechuan alone, in the
period of January to September, 1953, 40,000 disputes were settled by Conciliation Commissions
within 117 hsien (counties).[31] The Commissions
engaged mainly in solving various civil disputes.
For example, in the district of Wei Hsien, province of Shantung, among 507 disputes settled by
the Commissions, 167 were land disputes, 198 family quarrels, 101 marriage and divorce cases, 21
inheritance, and 20 debt disputes.[32]. According
to the report by Shih Liang, Minister of Justice,
there were 157,966 Conciliation Commissions in
China up to July 1955.[33]

The Intermediate Courts and Higher Courts. The
Intermediate Courts are found in the comparatively
large cities and autonomous regions, and are at
the intermediate level between the lower courts and
the courts on the highest level.[34] The Intermediate
Courts hear cases of the first instance assigned

173

by law or decrees to their jurisdiction or referred to them by the Basic Courts. As for cases of the second instance, they hear appeals and protests of the decisions of the inferior courts.[35] The courts on the intermediate level also have the right to request transfer of important civil and criminal cases to upper courts for trial.[36] The Higher Courts hear cases transferred to them by Intermediate Courts.

The Organic Law of the People's Courts increased the levels of the local courts by two instead of one. Unlike the Provisional Regulations of the Organization of the People's Court, the Law does not provide for any affiliates or divisions of the courts in the district of the court's jurisdiction. The internal organization of both the Intermediate and Higher Courts is, by law, similarly regulated: They are composed of a president, one or two vice-presidents, several chiefs of divisions, deputy chiefs, and the judges.[37] A division of civil cases and a division of criminal cases are included in both Courts.[38] In practice, the composition of the courts also included groups for examining certain specific cases. For example, at the beginning of the planned economic construction, special groups have been created within the courts of provincial and city level for the examining of cases related to national economic program.[39]

"Judicial Committees" have been established at the local people's courts. The main task of the committees is to discuss the important and complicated cases as well as other questions of judicial work.[40] Cases are referred to the committees for review by the president of the court in instances where a decision, after having acquired legal validity, was found to contain an erroneous evaluation of circumstances or application of the law.[41] Members of judicial committees of local courts are appointed by the people's councils at the corresponding levels, and committee

174

members of the Supreme People's Court are appointed by the Standing Committee of the NPC.[42] Meetings of judicial committees of people's courts are presided over by the presidents of the courts and frequently the chief procurators present and participate in the discussions. The committees are the important organs of Party control within the court. They provide guidance in policy and principles of legality in trial.

The Supreme Court. The Supreme People's Court is the highest judicial institution in Communist China. It is invested with the power of supervision over the judicial work of the local and special courts.[43] It hears the appeals both from lower courts and Supreme People's Procuratorate. The 1951 Regulations give the Supreme Court the power to retry cases "in accordance with (its) leadership and supervisory functions" in which "serious errors" were found in the judgment.[44] The Court was empowered by the 1954 Organic Law to take cognizance of any cases it considers that it should try.[45] Since the Supreme Court is responsible to the National People's Congress and the president of the Court is "elected" by the NPC,[46] it should by no means be considered as independent or the highest court, in practice.

Special Courts. The Organic Law of the People's Courts provides for three categories of special courts: Military Courts, Railway-Transport Courts, and Water-Transport Courts.[47] The special transport courts are given the jurisdiction to hear cases of counter-revolutionary activities, such as plundering, bribery, sabotage, indifference to duty resulting in serious damage to production or government property, and a threat to the safety of rail and water transport workers and employees.[48] The sessions of the special transport court are usually attended by a large number of railway and water transport workers, and the court decisions are widely discussed. For example, the session of the Harbin Railway Transport Court, hearing the case of Yuan-hua Kao,[49] was attended by 1,600 workers, and after watching the trial, the worker's meeting examined the situation and resolved to observe the rules and to be firmly disciplined.[50] It is obvious that these courts are used to perform disciplinary and educational functions in factories and industrial areas.

Military courts include legal organs of the People's Liberation Army and the former military tribunals of the Military Control Committees. During the early days of the regime, the military tribunals were used extensively as substitutes for the ordinary courts. These courts were gradually replaced after the judicial reform of 1954.

Legal organs of the army have a hierarchy of their own, including a Supreme Military Court under the Minister of Defense. Despite the Constitutional provision giving the Supreme People's Court supervisory jurisdiction over Military Courts, these courts have remained independent. They handle cases of international espionage involving non-military as well as military personnel.[51]

Another group of special courts — the Comrade Worker Courts — were neither mentioned in the Constitution nor in the Organic Law, but were established by the Judicial Conference of 1953. These courts are also known as Comrades' Adjudication Committees designed for the workers' "self-education and self-reform".[52] They are not technically considered legal organs although they perform legal functions. Like the Transportation Courts, they are used by the party to correct disciplinary problems such as absenteeism and lateness in various enterprises. The sessions of Comrade Courts are presided by a trial panel, composed of eleven to thirty-nine members. A judge from the local people's court is also present to give necessary legal advice. These courts are similar to the Comradely Courts of the U.S.S.R., which were formed in industrial areas. In the

176

Soviet Union, they have the power to fine and to issue reprimands and public censure. The Comrade Worker Courts deal with matters of less significance than do the Transportation Courts.

Neighborhood Committees or Street Committees are similar quasi-judicial organizations. They are organized in all streets and neighborhoods, and concern themselves with the matters from public hygiene to marriage registration. They have subcommittees for law and order and the district court provides a manual to help these committees. Residents of the areas are urged to attend the meetings and attempt to resolve local and family problems there, so formal litigation can be avoided.[53]

The organization of the special court has not been defined by the Organic Law of the People's courts. The Standing Committee of the National People's Congress was empowered to prescribe the organization of these courts and quasi-judicial institutions[54] and the Supreme People's Court has supervisory jurisdiction over them.[55]

All courts throughout the world serve, to a certain extent, an educational purpose. But in China the educational role of courts has been emphasized to an unprecedented degree. As early as in the Second Congress of Chinese Soviets in 1934, Mao Tse-tung emphasized the need for reformatory education for prisoners. After the judicial reform of 1954, the educational role of the courts is even written into the Organic Law of the People's Courts, which made legal the obligation of courts to educate the citizenry towards partiotism and a conscious respect for law.[56] The educational role is performed by the people's courts through the methods of public trials, publication of courts proceedings and decisions, labor reform, group discussion, mass self-criticism, and confession.[57]

The Provisional Regulations contain no mention of the independent administration of justice pro-

177

claimed in the Article 4 of the Organic Law of the People's Courts. Although the political system of Communist China denies the doctrine of separation of powers, the Organic Law expressly provides that the courts administer justice subject only to law.[58] This point deserves some discussion, but it should be notices that the Provisional Regulations stated clearly that in the absence of enacted laws, etc., the courts must base their decisions on "the policy of the Central People's Government". The principle of "judicial independence" dates from the Constitution of 1954. What does it signify? Of course, all bourgeois theories of the separation of powers are repudiated. It has been remarked that the judicial independence proclaimed is not, as in the Soviet Union, the independence of judges, but the independence of the Courts in the manner that judges are answerable to the bodies that elect or appoint them;[59] a lower court cannot be ordered by a higher court for a decision making.[60] This does not mean that the judges and the courts are independent from the Government and the Party.

Finally, the People's Courts "administer justice, subject only to the Law". But where is the law to be found, especially with the lack of civil and criminal codifications?

The People's
Procuratorates

Communist China appears to have imported from the Soviet Union the system of procuracy, a basic feature of socialist legality instituting complete control by the executive over all stages of judicial processes. Early in 1949, the Organic Law of the Central People's Government[61] directed that the Central People's Government Council should set up the People's Procurator-General's Office as the highest organ of the procuratorate in the country.[62]

178

It is prescribed that the Central People's Government Council should also exercise the authority of appointment and removal of the Procurator-General, his deputies, and the members of the People's Procurator-General's Office.[63] Prior to the adoption of the Constitution, the procuratorate was under the dual leadership of its own superior organs and the government council of the corresponding level of authority.[64] This was considered realistic during the "Three-anti" and "Five-anti" period.[65] The Provisional Procuratorate Regulations of 1951 permitted the procuratorate to take part in important cases[66] and gave it the power to protest a court judgment and to appeal to a higher court.[67] The people's procurator could investigate any individual citizen as well as government organs in order to ensure strict observance of the law, and if violations were found, prosecution could be instituted.[68]

The duty to investigate counter-revolutionaries, protest unwarranted judgments and institute prosecution were provisionally entrusted to public security organs under the supervision of the people's procurators. The administration of the office of the Procurator-General was highly centralized. The Provisional Procuratorate Regulations indicated that a Councillors' Conference of the Procurator-General's Office was to be held monthly to decide upon policy.[69] If this conference was not in unanimous agreement on a particular issue, the opinion of the Procurator-General was regarded as the deciding vote.

Lenin believes that the procurator's office must be "under the closest supervision and in the most immediate contact with three party institutions which constitute the maximum guarantee against local and individual influences: The Organization Bureau of the Central Committee, The Political Bureau of the Central Committee, and The Central Control Committee."[70] Especially the Central Committee of the party should maintain the closest

179

relationship with the Procuratorates. The Constitution of the Communist Party of China indicates:

> The tasks of the central and local commissions are as follows: regularly to examine and deal with cases of violation of the Party Constitution, party discipline, communist ethics and the state laws and decrees on the part of Party members; to decide on or cancel disciplinary measures against Party members; and to deal with appeals and complaints from Party members.[71]

This constitutional provision of the party duplicates the power of the Procuratorates. They have almost the same functions as the control committee of the party.[72] As a state organ, the people's procuratorate is just as important in checking upon governmental officials as the party's control committee used to check upon party members.[73] The Procurator-Generals have always been members of the Central Control Committee of the Communist Party.

The Constitution of 1954 provided that: "In the exercise of their authority local organs of the people's procuratorate are independent and not subject to interference by local organs of State."[74] The Constitution elevated the position and increased the power of the procuratorate. Unlike the courts, which are responsible to the people's congress of corresponding levels, all procurators are directly responsible to the Procurator-General,[75] who alone is responsible to the People's Congress or, when it is not in session, to its Standing Committee.[76] The Organic Law of the Procuratorates further provided that the Procurator-General is authorized to attend the meetings of the Judicial Committee of the Supreme Court and to participate in the proceedings. "If he does not agree to any decision of the Judicial Committee, he has the power to refer it to the Standing

Committee fo the National People's Congress for examination and decision."[77]

The procuratorates have the responsibility of investigating as well as prosecuting criminal cases. This investigation is of special importance in the legal system of Communist China because the evidence to support a criminal charge must be proved to the satisfaction of the court before the charge is laid. The evidence, prepared by the procurator in written form, then becomes the basis for the proceedings at the trial. The procuratorate also may intervene in civil cases affecting the public interest.

The Organic Law gave the procuratorate the authority to protest a "legally effective" judgment or to request an appeal of a case.[78] Arrest of any citizen requires the approval of the procuratorate, except for cases in which it has been authorized by a court.[79] The judge, who is subject to the supervisory power of the procuratorate, reads the charge presented by the procurator and questions the accused as to the validity of the charges. Since the procuratorate represents the "people" and informed by the "people", and since the "people" cannot be wrong, an accused in a criminal case is presumed guilty.[80] If the procurator disagrees with the court's decision, he may either appeal it immediately or request annulment of the judgment as being in error. The accused might be defended by an attorney, but the people's lawyer is a member of the State Counsel Office and is, therefore, responsible for upholding State policy, so he is not likely to oppose the procurator too vigorously.

The Procuratorates may not, however, directly interfere with the administration of the government.[81] But the powerful influence and the effectiveness of the Procuratorates should not be underestimated. In 1956, for example, a total of 1,400 court decisions were protested by the Procuratorates and 1,159 were either appealed or received for new trials.[82]

In a report submitted by Tseng Ch'ang-ming, Chief Procurator of Kwangtung Province, to the Third Kwangtung People's Congress, it appeared that the guiding policy for procuratorial work was being streamlined to the extent that justice had become a secondary consideration to speed during the 1958 "big leap forward". Speaking of the result obtained from experimental "laboratories" in the City of Canton, Mr. Tseng reported:

> The result of the experiments was spectacular: without sacrificing efficiency in work and with due respect to legal procedure, we were able to shake off the fetters of old practices and do away with 32 kinds of unnecessary procedures. Now, on the average only 3 hours are required to dispose of a case, involving all procedures in effecting arrest, examination of evidence, and prosecution at the court. As compared with the pre-rectification record, the new method raised the efficiency of work several score of times.[83]

Thus, in equating speed with efficiency, the Chief Procurator of Kwangtung gave further explanation:

> Speed means swiftness in approving arrests, approving each case promptly as it turns up. In ordinary circumstances, decisions should be scrutinized promptly as they come up; in ordinary cases, it shall not take more than 24 hours for completion of scrutiny at the procuratorate and prosecution at the court after filing a case.[84]

The Procuratorates of Communist China, though patterned upon the Soviet model, could actually trace its genesis to the censorate of Imperial

China.[85] The traditional Chinese censorate was
designed to serve as the eyes and ears of the Emperor. The imperial censors were dispatched to
all parts of the country to receive appeals from
the commoners for mistried cases and to investigate any corruption among government officials and
report directly to the Emperor. This system acquired such an entrenched position in the traditional government structure that Dr. Sun Yat-sen
decided to retain its main features in the Control
Yuan.[86] The Nationalist Government, however, did
not make effective use of this constitutional check
upon the other four government powers, the Executive, the Legislative, the Judicial, and the Examination. It is yet too soon to predict whether
the Chinese Communists would properly utilize the
Procuratorates as the censorial check upon government authorities and as the judicial safeguard
in protecting citizen's rights. But it is certain that the Procuratorates of Communist China
was, and is, a very powerful institution and has
great influence upon the legal system.

The Lawyer

The legal profession in traditional Chinese society
never attained the same status and importance as it
has in the West. This may be attributed to the elevation of the Confucianist concept of li over the
Legalist emphasis of fa. A western-style judicial
system was instituted after the establishment of
the Republic and the legal profession was introduced.

The quality of justice depends on a multitude
of factors. The form and substance of law, the
organization of the courts, the litigants' common
knowledge of law, and in particular, his ability
to utilize this legal knowledge all have an important bearing on the administration of justice.
The ordinary litigants in Chinese society were

mostly ignorant of the law, especially modern civil law. The other factor on which the quality of modern justice depends is the quality of the bench and the bar. Modern court procedure makes the service of the attorney almost indispensable. Unfortunately, in China the legal profession has developed slowly, few qualified law school graduates have been admitted to the bar, and not all who have been admitted are well qualified by training and by standards of legal ethics. In the larger cities the corporations and industrial commerce provided for the legal profession a suf- amount of practices. For the countryside or the smaller cities, the lawyer has no way of making a living and is practically non-existent. In short, neither the quality nor the competence of the lawyer in China could receive the same pres- tige and respect as in the Western societies.

After the establishment of the Communist gov- ernment, the Kuomintang laws were abolished, but new laws were slow in coming. There was almost no law text for the law schools to teach,[87] and lawyers as a class were regarded as tools of the bourgeois capitalists and imperialists. The Chinese Communists in the early years maintained the traditional hostile and suspicious attitude toward the legal profession. Law offices were closed, and private lawyers were prohibited from practicing.[88] There was a serious doubt as to whether lawyers would ever have a place in the New Democracy.

On the other hand, the government of Commun- ist China continued to recognize officially the accused's right to defense in a lawsuit. Refer- ence also was made to the preparation of the in- troduction of a system of people's lawyers. For example, the "Provisional Regulations of the Shanghai People's Court Governing the Disposal of Civil and Criminal Cases" provided that the accused in a criminal case is entitled to have a public defense counsel.[89] In a civil case, the litigants might, with the permission of the presiding judge, designate their closest relative as legal agents to appear in court.[90] A simialr provision on the right of defense was expressed in the Organic Regulations of People's Tribunals that; "When a hsien (county) people's tribunal and its branches conduct a trial, they shall guarantee the right of the accused to defend himself and to have defense counsel must be approved by the Tribunal before he can argue the case."[91]

In his report, Hsu Te-heng, the Acting Chairman of the Law Codification Committee, stated that "in an open trial, the litigants and their approved counsels should be given full rights of voice and defense."[92] The Communist official pronounced that in order to "manifest the democratic spirit of our judicial work and to protect the right of defense for the accused as well as the legitimate interest of the civil litigants. We have instituted public defenders to perform for the accused or one of the litigant parties such tasks as gathering evidence, examining the circumstances of the case, studying problems, and taking part in the trial in order that experience can be accumulated to establish a new system of people's lawyer."[93] Undoubtedly, some efforts and progress had been made in the early years in the direction of introducing people's attorneys to China.

Contrary to what was legally guaranteed, the common practice was that the accused yielded and confessed his guilt. Neither in the trials nor in the testimonies given by Chinese as well as foreign witnesses was there a single case in the pre-constitutional period where the accused was defended by himself or by a defense attorney.[94] Speaking from personal experience, Father Bonnichon, former Dean of the Law faculty at the University L'Aurore of Shanghai explained the "right to defense" in the Communist Chinese court:

...not only is the accused presumed guilty, but he is forbidden to prove the contrary: to try, is to revolt.... In the presence of such a conception of procedure, can we be astonished at the complete suppression of lawyers? The conception is rooted in the logic of the system, and the services of a lawyer before such tribunals becomes not only superfluous but absolutely unthinkable. *Defense amounts to revolt.* Who would dare, even as a lawyer appointed by law, to oppose the "government" in the defense of an accused. The words of the lawyer would die in his throat and he would feel equally as guilty as his client. The absence of defense counsel in the criminal process is not, therefore, accidental, but, on the contrary, imperatively solicited by the fundamental conceptions of Communist penal law.[95]

Former private lawyers in China already banned from practice of law received a further purge when the Communist government launched Judicial Reform during 1953 and 1954. It should be noted that although the Communist government abolished the legal system of the Kuomintang, it was forced to retain many of the old judges and lawyers because of the shortage of cadres trained in law. Having had only a brief experience of Communist indoctrination, these former Kuomintang judges and lawyers understandably still kept much of their traditional legal concepts and practices.[96] Thus, one of the main objectives of the Judicial Reform was to purge and to liquidate the *hei lu-shih* (underground lawyers). Since the "liberation", lawyers had been compelled to give up their practice. Many of them had set up offices to handle accounting, or to draw up documents for people in urban areas. Others had become trustees, managers, or secretaries in private enterprises.

However, some, the Communists charged, had been using their new positions as a screen to carry on "underground" law practice. Their illegal acts, according to official reports, included bribery and corruption, fraud and blackmail, perversion of justice, monopoly of lawsuits, incitement to strifes and disputes.[97] These "underground lawyers" were required to register with the people's courts and to make their "confessions".[98]

The 1954 Constitution marked the beginning of a more orderly development in the legal life of Communist China. When the turmoil changed into reasonable political stability and economic construction, a reversal of the attitude toward lawyers became gradually noticeable. The right to defense was among those deomcratic legal guarantees clearly provided by the Constitution: "The accused has the right to defense."[99] The Organic Law of the People's Courts has a similar provision: "The accused, besides personally defending his case, may designate advocates (lawyers) to defend it, or have it defended by a citizen recommended by a people's organization or approved by the people's court, or defined by a near relative or guardian. The people's court may also, when it deems necessary, appoint a counsel for the accused."[100] Hailing the new lawyer as protector of people's rights and guardian of the New Democracy, even the *Guide to Higher Education* urged the best brains to enter the law schools: "We must esteem and protect the new lawyer!"[101]

The first indication that new lawyers became a part of the legal system in Communist China was the official announcement on November 23, 1954 the decision of the Military Tribunal of the Supreme Court on thirteen Americans involved in two alleged espionage cases. The Communist government appointed two law professors of the China People's University[102] as defense counsels for the accused.[103] Lawyers were introduced in thirty-three courts in 1955[104] and the system of defense counsel on trial had been enforced by the Ministry of Justice in Shanghai, Peking, Wuhan, and other major cities.[105] The newly trained Communist lawyers began to discuss the drafts of the "Regulations for Lawyers" and of the "Provisional Rules for Lawyers' Fees". According to the Minister of Justices report in 1957, there were lawyers in most cities to act as people's legal advisers. There were some 2,000 fulltime lawyers and 700 Legal Advisory Offices throughout the country.[106] Undlubtedly, the number of lawyers is still too small, and they are practicing only in large cities. But the fact that the Communist government now permits lawyers to practice is an important change in its legal system.

People's bar has been organized in the cities of Shanghai, Peking, and Tientsin.[107] The function and organization of the people's bar is regulated by the "Provisional Rules for Lawyers", drafted in 1957 by the Ministry of Justice, but nothing has been said publicly since.[108] Lawyers in Communist China are organized into Bar Associations throughout provinces, autonomous regions, and municipalities directly under the central authority. Neither a state organ nor a private group, the Association is a voluntary social organization within the broad framework of the judicial system and accepts the guidance and control of the judicial organs of the state. Under the Bar Association, there are Legal Advisory Offices in counties and cities to handle some lawyer's routine work, e.g., giving legal information and advice to the citizens.

It is interesting to note that the requirements for admission to the people's bar are rather irregular; no bar examination is required. According to the regulations, a citizen who has the right to vote and be elected and who meets one of the following three conditions may apply for membership to a Bar Association: (1) a graduate from a university law school or a secondary law school of Communist China with at least one year judicial experience; (2) a former judge or procurator for at least one year service in a people's court or a people's procuratorate; and (3) a person with certain cultural standard (educational background), legal knowledge, and social experience suitable to the practice of law.[109] After the board of directors of the Bar Association approves his membership, he is then assigned to a Legal Advisory Office to serve as a people's lawyer. Social science professors, deputies of the People's Congresses, or officials of various people's organizations may concurrently serve as part-time lawyers if admitted to a Bar Association.[110]

In Communist China, lawyers are not private legal professionals but public servants. There are no private law offices in the cities since they all work in Legal Advisory Offices. Fees are paid by clients to the Legal Advisory Office rather than individual lawyers. At times, free service must be rendered if the client proves too poor to pay, is involved in pension or alimony claims, or has other justifiable reasons.[111] Lawyers receive their salaries from the Legal Advisory Offices where they practice collectively. The scale is set by the Bar Association according to the ability and the amount of work of each individual lawyer.[112]

In civil cases, a lawyer, as a representative for the plaintiff, defendant, or other parties, is allowed in Communist China to make himself as the mandate (delegation of power) in either written or an oral form by the party.[113] According to the legal system of Communist China, the defense counsel is not an agent of the defendent in a criminal proceeding. He is an independent party in the trial and is not bound by the will of the defendant. He must honestly perform his duties within a legal framework, and under no circumstances should he fabricate evidence, distort facts, or use deceptions to help his client.

If the crime has been established beyond any doubt, the counsel should only defend the accused from the standpoint of certain extenuating circumstances, such as the motives, objective reason for the crime, the degree of his repentance, etc.[114]

The Chinese press has frequently reported cases in which the accused were defended by lawyers. But most of these cases were ordinary — civil and non-political in nature. With exceptions, the presence of defense counsels was reported at the trials of "espionage" cases in 1954 and 1960, one involving thirteen Americans and the other Bishops James Walsh and Kung P'in-mei.[115] However, no details were given by the press. It is doubtful whether the lawyers in both trials did more than serve a propaganda purpose.

Basically, the position of the defense counsel in criminal trials is very closely related to the position of the courts in the overall structure of the state. The position of the courts, in turn, is directly related to the fundamental principles on which the state is founded — that is, to the basic concepts of law, justice, and the relationship between state and citizen.

Since it is the duty of the court to determine the degree of guilt as a measure of the penalty to be imposed, it becomes the duty of the defense counsel to present all facts and circumstances favorable to his client, provided that, in so doing, he does not compromise the allegiance he owes to the ruling ideology and the state. It is not easy to say precisely how far an attorney can go in defending an accused without opening his own political loyalty to question. If he contests the specifications of the indictment, he puts himself in opposition to the prosecutor, who is both a state official and a party member; if he appeals the conviction of his client, he challenges the correctness of the decision of the court, which is a state agency. These concerns

obviously impose restraints upon his freedom of
action in conducting the defense of his client.

One of the problems confronting the people's
lawyer is the existence of many gaps in Chinese
law. While a few fundamental statutes have been
promulgated, there is no complete civil code,
criminal code, or code of procedure in the People's
Republic. The practicing lawyer can find his
work extremely difficult in cases where there
are no codifications to rely on. Another problem
besetting the people's lawyer is the unfriendly
attitude sometimes shown by the judicial personnel.
Since the system of legal defense is still in its
infancy, there is a tendency on the part of many
judges and procurators to treat defense counsels
with hostility and contempt. Some regard them
as subordinates and some feel that the presence
of a lawyer at a trial is a "nuisance" and a
"waste of time".[116] Furthermore, the government
of Communist China expects that the people's
lawyer should put his duty to the State above
his duty to the defendant.[117]

The attitude of people's lawyers with respect
to the observance of professional secrecy illus-
trates the point. In all democratic countries,
lawyers are legally entitled to refuse to disclose any information confidentially given to
them by their clients.[118] Chinese Communist law,
on the contrary, does not recognize any right of
"confidential communication" between a lawyer
and his client: like all other citizens of Communist China, lawyers have the formal duty to
co-operate with the state judicial organs in
combating criminality. In fact, however, most
lawyers choose to close their eyes to this duty
rather than act in such a way as to undermine
the confidential relationship between themselves
and their clients.

This situation has prompted Chinese journals
to lecture to members of the bar on the difference
between the Western and Chinese Communist concepts

of professional ethics for lawyers.[119] Whereas the bourgeois lawyers' ethics sanctions the "right to lie" on behalf of a criminal, one article asserted, "socialist morality" demands that the people's lawyer exclusively serve the cause of truth.[120] From time to time, the Chinese press has also carried reports of alleged "anti-moral" conduct on the part of members of the legal profession. The publicity given to such cases is evidently aimed at forcing lawyers into a more compliant role as defenders of socialist justice.

The position of the lawyer in Communist China is still at an experimental stage and is being tried in a new evolving Communist society. The irregularities and handicaps under which Chinese lawyers have to practice, in fact, reflect the unsettled status of the people's bar as well as that of the legal system of Communist China.

NOTES

1. See *Organic Law of the People's Courts of the People's Republic of China* and *Organic Law of the People's Procuratorates of the People's Republic of China,* both adopted by the First Session of the First National People's Congress on September 21, 1954. English texts can be found in Blaustein, *Fundamental Legal Documents of Communist China* (South Hackensack, New Jersey: Fred B. Rothman & Co., 1962), pp. 131-143; 144-150. Hereinafter cited as *Organic Law of the Courts; Organic Law of the Procuratorates.*

2. Also known as the Comrade Worker Courts, designed for the workers' self-education and self-reform. See *Current Background,* No. 349 (August 25, 1955), p. 2.

3. *Fukien Jih Pao* (Fukien Daily), January 15, 1957, p. 4.

4. Figure used in Subhash Chandra Sarkar's article, "Judiciary in China", *India Quarterly* No. 13 (1957), p. 308. The author indicated that that figure was supplied by T. K. Cheng of the Foreign Language Press in Peking.

5. Article 7, *The Common Programme*.

6. Article 27, *The Common Programme*.

7. Article 18, *The Common Programme*.

8. See L. M Gudoshnikov, *Legal Organs of The People's Republic of China*, English translation by JPRS (1698-N), p. 28.

9. These figures were reported by the Minister of Justice, Shih Liang, at the First All-China Conference of Judicial Workers, August 3, 1950, "Collected Reports of the Work of the People's Government in 1950", p. 99. Quoted in *ibid*.

10. Text can be found in *Current Background*, No. 183 (May 26, 1952). Hereinafter cited as *Provisional Court Regulations*.

11. *People's Daily*, August 30, 1952.

12. The principle regulations for the reform were contained in the report by the Minister of Justice Shih Liang, adopted by the State Council as a guide for the judicial reform. *People's Daily*, August 13, 1952.

13. Literally translated as "Three-anti" (1951-1952): anti-corruption, anti-waste, and anti-bureaucratism.

14. Literally translated as "Five-anti" (1952): anti-bribery, anti-tax-evasion, anti-fraud, anti-theft of state property, and anti-theft of state economic information. See Franklin W. Houn, *To Change A Nation: Propaganda and Indoctrination in Communist China* (Glencoe: Free Press, 1961).

15. *People's Daily*, August 23, 1953. For more information on judicial training of a people's judge, see Re-bing Gurr, "How I Learned To Be a Judge", *Political-Legal Research,* No. 3 (1965), pp. 26-27.

16. *Ibid.*

17. Article 1, *Organic Law of the Courts.*

18. Documents of the First Session of the First National People's Congress of the People's Republic of China, (Peking: Foreign Language Press, 1955), p. 187; and Article 2, *Ibid.*

19. Article 32, *Organic Law of the Courts.*

20. *Ibid.*

21. Article 18, *Organic Law of the Courts.*

22. *Ibid.*

23. Article 15, *Organic Law of the Courts.*

24. *People's Daily*, July 21, 1954.

25. *Ibid.*

26. Text can be found in *FKHP*, Vol. 4 (1957), pp. 295-298. Hereinafter cited as *Act of Conciliation.*

27. Article 2, 4, *Act of Conciliation*.

28. Article 5, *ibid*.

29. Article 6, *ibid*.

30. Article 8, *ibid*.

31. *People's Daily*, March 23, 1954, p. 1.

32. *Ibid*., p. 3.

33. *People's Daily*, July 30, 1955, p. 6.

34. Article 20, *Organic Law of the Courts*.

35. Article 22, *Organic Law of the Courts*.

36. *Ibid*.

37. Articles 21 and 24, *Organic Law of the Courts*.

38. *Ibid*. These divisions correspond to the collegiums of courts in the Soviet Union.

39. In the summer 1955, there were 120 such groups. See Pi-wu Tung's address before the Second Session of the National People's Congress, *Hsin-hua Yueh-pao (New China Monthly)*, No. 8 (July 1955), p. 60.

40. Article 10, *Organic Law of the Courts*.

41. Article 12, *ibid*.

42. Article 10, *ibid*.

43. Article 14, *ibid*.

44. Article 28, *Provisional Court Regulations*.

45.   Article 30, *Organic Law of the Courts.*

46.   Articles 14, 32, *ibid.;* see also Article 10, Organic Law of the National People's Congress.

47.   Article 26, *Organic Law of the Courts.*

48.   See Resolution adopted by the Second All-Chinese Conference of Judicial Workers in *FKHP,* Vol. 2 (1955), p. 95.

49.   Yuan-hua Kao, a railroad worker, violated the rules of the technical operation which resulted in a train collision in March 1954.

50.   *People's Daily,* September 4, 1954.

51.   See Henry Wei, "Courts and Police in Communist China", Studies in Chinese Communism (Series I, No. 1), Human Resources Institute, Air University, (Montgomery, Alabama), 1955.

52.   See *China News Analysis,* No. 31 (April 9, 1954); note 2, *supra.*

53.   "A Day at Street Committee," *Kwang-chow Jih Pao* (Canton Daily), March 2, 1957.

54.   Article 27, *Organic Law of the Courts.*

55.   Article 28, *ibid.*

56.   Article 3, *ibid.*

57.   The requirement of a confession prior to conviction was a characteristic of the traditional Chinese law. For the Chinese Communists, confession contributes to the establishment of limits of investigation and collection of evidence for the crime and aid the court, the procurator's office, and the police in handling cases. Confes-

sion also makes it possible to determine the degree of the repentance of the accused and his moral qualities. Tse-pei Cheng, "Correct Attitude Towards the Confession of the Accused", *Kuang-ming Daily* (November 13, 1956), p. 3.

58. Article 4. *Organic Law of the Courts*.

59. Articles 32, 33, 34, *Organic Law of the Courts*.

60. K'un-lin Liu "On Independence of Courts, Subject Only to Law", *Political-Legal Research* No. 1 (1955), pp. 35-40.

61. Adopted by the First Plenary Session of the Chinese People's PCC on September 29, 1949 in Peking. Text can be found in Blaustein, *op. cit.*, pp. 104-114. Hereinafter cited as *Organic Law of the Government*.

62. Article 5, *Organic Law of the Government*.

63. Article 7, *ibid*.

64. See "Explanatory Report on the Office of People's Procurator-General", *Current Background*, No. 183 (May 26, 1952), p. 19.

65. *Ibid*.

66. Article 36, *Provisional Procuratorate Regulations*.

67. Article 30, *ibid*.

68. Article 3, *ibid*.

69. Article 6, *ibid*.

70. Quoted in Andrei Y. Vyshinsky, *The Law of the Soviet State*, translated by Hugh W. Babb (New York: MacMillan, 1948), p. 526.

71. Article 53.

72. See Ching-yao Yen, "How China Is Governed", *People's China* No. 1 (January 1955), p. 14.

73. The control committee are centralized agencies of the Central Executive Committee used to check upon Party members. See Franz Michael, "Communist China's First Decade: The Party", *New Leader* (April 6, 1959).

74. Article 83 of the *Constitution*.

75. Article 6, *Organic Law of the Procuratorates*.

76. Article 7, *ibid.*; cf. Article 84 of the *Constitution*.

77. Article 17, *Organic Law of the Procuratorates*.

78. Articles 8, 9, 10, 11, *ibid.*

79. Article 12, *ibid.*

80. See, for example, Bonnichon, "Law in Communist China", *International Commission of Jurists,* 1955, p. 8, who quotes the following speech he claims in given to every accused: "You are guilty because the government has not arrested you without considerable investigation and deliberation."

81. Article 8, *Organic Law of the Procuratorates*.

82. *FKHP*, Vol. 6, p. 291.

83. *Canton Daily*, May 26, 1958.

84. *Ibid*.

85. For this particular discussion, see Charles O. Hucker, "The Traditional Chinese Censorate and the New Peking Regime," *The American Political Science Review*, Vol. 45 (1951), pp. 1041-1057.

86. Under the Nationalist Government, Control Yuan is one of the Five Separation of Powers. (The others: Executive, Legislative, Judicial, and Examination Yuan).

87. The 1953 *Guide to Higher Institutions* listed only one School (Chungshan University, Canton) offering law degrees.

88. The Ministry of Justice ordered in 1950 the suppression of the activity of private lawyers. See "Strictly Prohibit the Illegal Activities of the Underground Lawyers", *People's Daily* (September 14, 1952).

89. Article 12. Text can be found in *Shen Pao* (Shanghai News), August 12, 1949.

90. *Ibid*.

91. Article 6. Text can be found in *Jen-min Shou-ts'e (The People's Handbook*, 1951), pp. 46-48.

92. "Explanatory Report on Provisional Organic Regulations of the People's Courts of the Chinese People's Republic," *People's Daily*, September 5, 1951.

93. "People's Judicial Reconstruction in the Past Two Years", *Hsin-hua Pan-yueh-k'an (New China Bi-Weekly)*, No. 19, Vol. 14, (October 1, 1951), p. 10.

94. Henry Wei, *op. cit.*, Chapters III, IV, and V.

95. Bonnichon, *op. cit.*, pp. 8-11.

96. See Shih Liang's "Report Concerning the Reform and Reorganization of the People's Courts at All Levels", in *Chang-chiang Daily* (Hankow, August 24, 1952).

97. *Ch'ang-chiang Daily* (September 9, 1952); *People's Daily* (September 14, 1952).

98. There were 780 "underground lawyers" had registered and "confessed" in Shanghai and 86 in Canton during the first month of the campaign. *People's Daily*, September 14, 1952.

99. Article 76, the *Constitution*.

100. Article 7, *Organic Law of the Courts*.

101. The 1954 *Guide to Higher Education* severely criticized the prevalent notion among high achool students: "Boys study engineering; girls learn medicine," but "those who are inferior, seek after politics and law." p. 143.

102. The Law School of the China People's University was the first law school of the Communist regime, established in 1950. It offered Soviet jurisprudence under the direction of Soviet legal experts. The School also translated Russian law texts and references and pioneered in the development of the Chinese legal education system. It's graduates become pro-

fessors at many law schools as well as many judicial organs. See *Political-Legal Research*, No. 2 (1954), pp. 74-75.

103. *People's Daily*, November 24, 1954.

104. *Kuang-ming Daily*, March 24, 1955.

105. Shih Liang, Speech before the NPC on July 29, 1955, *Current Background*, No. 349 (August 25, 1955), p. 14.

106. *Kuang-ming Daily*, January 1, 1957. See also Felix Greene, *Awakened China* (Garden City, New York: Doubleday) p. 194.

107. There is no detailed direct information available on the people's bar. But, the general functions and organization may be gleaned from a description of the Soviet bar. See Ju-chi Wang, "The Functions and Organization of Soviet Attorneys", *Political-Legal Research*, No. 6 (1955), p. 26.

108. For some incomplete text of the Provisional Rules for Lawyers, see *Kuang-ming Daily*, June 17, 1957.

109. See *Jen-min shou-ts'e 1957 (People's Handbook)*, p. 337.

110. "Concerning the Question of the People's Lawyer System," *Kuang-ming Daily*, July 7, 1956; see also Kan-vu Wang, "Some Insights Gained From the Establishment of the New Lawyer System," *Political-Legal Research*, No. 2 (1956), p. 20.

111. See the Provisional Rules for Lawyers' Fees; text in *FKHP* Vol. 4 (1957), pp. 235-238.

112. *Ibid.*

113. *Basic Problems in the Civil Law*, p. **99**.

114. Pin-lin Chao, *et al*. "The Lawyer System and Criminal Procedure in Our Country." *Chiao-hsueh yu yen-chiu (Teaching and Research)* Peking, No. 23 (1955), p. 20; cf. Heng-yuan Chou, "On the Right to Defense of the Accused in the Criminal Procedure of Our Country," *Political-Legal Research*, No. 3 (1956), p. 51.

115. *Kuang-ming Daily*, November 23, 1954; September 18, 1960.

116. "A Few Words in Behalf of the People's Lawyer," *Kuang-ming Daily*, January 27, 1957.

117. See Jung-pin Cheng, "Lawyers Must Serve the Socialist Legal System," *Science of Law*, No. 2, (1958), pp. 36-38; Tzu-chiang Lin, "Thorough Criticism of Bourgeois Thinking in the Work of the People's Lawyers," *ibid.*,pp. 39-43; cf. P'u Chang, "Destroying Thoroughly the Old Legal System and Liquidating Bourgeois Legal Thinking," *Political-Legal Research*, No. 2 (1964), pp. 15-18.

118. For example, the criminal code of the Germen Federal Republic even makes it a punishable offense for the defense counsel in a criminal case to disclose "without authorization...private secrets confided to him by reason of his function." (Section 300).

119. See Mou Chang, "Thorough Separation from the Bourgeois Concept of Law," *Political-Legal Research*, No. 6 (1958). pp. 37-39; P'u Chang, *op. cit.*, pp. 15-17.

120. Tzu-chiang Lin, *op. cit.*

7   Conclusion

Law and State

There are areas in public affairs in which individual liberty inevitably comes into conflict with national security. But in a free society the ultimate solution to this conflict rests, in substantial measure, with an independent judiciary which is empowered, within limits, to review actions taken by the executive and the legislative branches of government. In Communist China, the position of the judiciary vis-à-vis the executive provides an interesting example of the opposite extreme. Supervision by the party is, in effect, complete control of the judiciary by the executive. The review of judicial decisions by the executive involves no special hearings. The power of "judicial review" by the executive provides an important means for the Communist Party to test the "accuracy" of judicial decisions in accordance with the State policy.

    The principle of legality as understood in a free society under the Rule of Law is expressed

in the subordination of state authorities to the
law and the consequent protection of citizens
against violation of the law and abuse of discretionary powers. Safeguards of legality, therefore, take the form of statutory provisions to
implement this subordination. These include
the existence of constitutional courts and administrative courts, judicial control over administrative action, and control of observance
of statutory requirements within the administration. A citizen whose rights or legitimate interests have been violated is legally entitled
to appeal to the guardians of constitutional and
administrative justice in order to obtain redress
and bring the State's supervisory machinery into
action. The legal system of Communist China
makes scarcely any provision for such recourse.

The legal position of the court, its function
and its strictly defined activity create favorable
conditions for ensuring the correct application
of legal norms as can no other form of state
activity. Therefore, within the system of legal
guarantees, judicial guarantees are the highest
guarantees of the rights of citizens. Hence,
one should draw the practical conclusion that
it is necessary to broaden the jurisdiction of
the court, to increase its role and prestige in
public life. In particular, the function of the
court should be extended to deal with the administrative activity of government agencies in
their relations with the population.

Chinese jurists insisted that the protection
of legality is primarily the task of the Procuratorate. The Procuratorate is supposedly the
guardian of legality in the whole field of administration and justice, although decisions by
the party fall outside its field. The citizen,
who cannot himself challenge a judicial decision
or an administrative act in due and proper form,
is supposedly entitled to take his grievance to
the Procuratorate. This is a request for what is

known as extra-legal redress. No attempt is made in practice. But, the Procuratorate's supervision of legality is effective only when the Party and state organs are concerned for the observance of the law.

The rules for interpreting the law, which the principle of legality requires to be applied scrupulously and predictably, are of vital importance in the maintenance of the principle of socialist legality. It is only too clear that legal interpretation is decisively influenced by the ideas, values, and aims underlying the legal system. According to the Chinese Communist concept, the law must also reflect the objective laws of human history in its progress towards a classless and stateless social order and must serve as an instrument in promoting and accelerating that process; that is to say, "in achieving socialist social relations." The organs of the State, including courts, are required to ensure that the law is applied in a manner "corresponding to the laws and needs of social evolution," in other words, to implement these conditions by applying the principle of Chinese Communist legality.

Being the vanguard of the working class, which is the latest class to appear in the course of history and, therefore, puts into execution the laws of history, the Communist Party is alone able to perceive whether social evolution follows these laws. Its decisions and lines for guidance are authoritative and binding on state organs which interpret and administer the law. Accordingly, all legal interpretation and the application of laws follow the Party. The Party's decisions and lines for guidance are also binding on judges, for whom freedom of judgment and independence are absolute requirements of the Rule of Law according to the Western pattern. The courts in Communist China are specifically designated as a part of the machinery for political guidance.

There is a fundamental divergence between the principle of communist law and the principle of law in State under the Rule of Law in their respective attitudes toward the individual. In the Western legal systems, the organs of the State are required to observe the laws in order to respect the individual freedom. Under the Chinese Communist legal system, not only is every individual required to adhere to the law, he must also collaborate actively in the implementation of socialist law.

The fact that every single individual comes within the operation of socialist legal system, thus, means that everyone is required to educate both himself and his fellows in order to become mature for the communist social order. In its extension and application to cover private individuals and their various relationships, the principle of Chinese socialist legality, as spelled out in communist legal doctrine, is an instrument of "social self-education." Thus, the legal system of Communist China differs from the legal system of the Rule of Law in this respect also: Its purpose is not to safeguard individual freedom but rather to permit the total shaping of the individual.

Theory v. Practice:
An Evaluation

Law in Chinese Communist legal theory is always functionally dynamic. The purpose of law is to change men and, as it fulfills this function, to undergo qualitative change itself. With the contraction of the judicial system as a whole, the theory is that legal rules will be transformed qualitatively into non-juridical moral standards. This in turn will lead to a concomitant expansion of the system of behavioral norms and habits identified in Chinese Communist literature as "rules of socialist community life," or the communist li.

206

The official newspaper of the Soviet Government has criticized the post-1957 Chinese legal system as a mockery of socialist legality.[1] American cold war rhetoric has long proclaimed the lawlessness of Chinese Communist rule. What conclusion should be reached by a detached evaluation? From the state's point of view, it can be argued that the contemporary law system of Communist China is not arbitrary in conception. The values and goals of the Chinese Communist state are protected by a body of communist li that prescribe a broad spectrum of behavior considered by the government to be anti-social. The communist li or rules of social behavior are enforced by a refined series of administrative and criminal sanctions and a comprehensive network of official and semiofficial institutions. These institutions, acting in accordance with their political orientations and party's policies, identify, apprehend, investigate, and judge those who are suspected of violating rules, and impose sanctions upon offenders. Both legal and extra-legal institutions act not only to suppress and punish offenders but also to reform them, to educate others, and to satisfy society's sense of just retribution.

After the Judicial Reform of 1954, the Chinese actually began to curb the power of police and other non-judicial agencies, and lead the People's Republic toward some degree of judicial independence. Obviously the legal system of Communist China lodges broad discretion in law enforcement officers and in the Party officials who approve important or difficult decisions but none of these authoritative persons is free to act without regard to a variety of principles that have been established to guide his discretion, and an appellate court is always available to review the exercise of that discretion.

In the criminal process the fate of the accused depends entirely on the degree of conscientiousness and ability of government and party

officials. The process has no place for independent actors who might defend the accused against
abuses committed by those who administer law. Even
certain aspects of the legal system that in theory
provide checks against abuses, in practice add to
its arbitrariness.

One of the most striking aspects of the legal
system of Communist China is the unusual importance
of mediation in the resolution of disputes. Adjudication and even arbitration are regarded as last
resorts in the People's Republic. Today's mainland
Chinese faithfully follow the preaching of Mao Tse-
tung that "disputes among the people' ought to be
resolved, whenever possible, by "democratic methods,
methods of discussion, of criticism, of persuasion
and education, not by coercive, oppresive methods."[2]
Most civil disputes between individuals are settled
by extra-judicial mediation.

The foreign observer is tempted to attribute
this to what he suspects must be the inevitable
impact, even upon radical revolutionaries, of mil-
lennial Confucian culture. He may find apparent
support in contemporary Chinese assertions that
mediation is "one of China's fine traditions."[3]
It would be premature to attempt to compare this
contemporary system with that of the past. Our
investigation does, however, suggest important
continuities between past and present. For example,
in extra-judicial and judicial practice under both
the Ching Dynasty and present systems in the words
of a communist slogan, "mediation is the main
thing, adjudication is secondary." This reflects
the fact that, even though there were vast differences between Confucianism and Maoism, each of
these dominant ideologies is hostile to litigation and places great emphasis upon "criticism-
education" and "self-criticism." It is also
tempting to view the Communists' new local elite
of party members, bureaucrats, policemen, union
activists and mediation committee members, and
other semi-officials as successors to the traditional gentry who settled most of the disputes.

Both in basic theories and in institutions and practices, there are some obvious similarities between the traditional and the Chinese Communist law systems. Many of these similarities derive from the great extent to which the interests of the Chinese state have always prevailed over those of the individual. A government of men, not of law; or a society of li rather than of law has deep roots in China. Thus, it has been assumed that the administration of justice is the exclusive preserve of the state, not of man.

NOTES

1. Quoted in Cohen *The Communism of Mao Tse-tung* (Chicago: The University of Chicago Press, 1964) p. 525.

2. Mao Tse-tung, "On the Correct Handling of Contradictions Among the People," (February 27, 1957), *FKHP*, Vol. I, pp. 5-6.

3. "Is It Necessary for Us to Retain the People's Mediation Committees?" *Kuang Ming Daily*, September 2, 1956.

Bibliography

Public Documents

People's Republic of China, *Common Programme of the Chinese People's Political Consultative Conference,* September 29, 1949.

People's Republic of China, *The Marriage Law,* May 1, 1950.

People's Republic of China, *People's Judicial Work,* Published by the People's Court of Peking, 1950.

People's Republic of China, *Provisional Organic Act of the People's Conciliation Commissions,* March 22, 1954.

People's Republic of China, *Constitution of the People's Republic of China,* September 20, 1954.

People's Republic of China, *Organic Law of the National People's Congress,* September 20, 1954.

People's Republic of China, *Organic Law of the People's Courts*, September 21, 1954.

People's Republic of Chine, *Organic Law of the People's Procuratorates*, September 21, 1954.

People's Republic of China, *Arrest and Detention Act*, December 31, 1954.

People's Republic of China, *Constitution of the Communist Party of China*, September 26, 1956.

Books

Archer, Peter, *Communism and the Law*. Dufour, England: Bodley Head, 1963.

Babb, Hugh (ed.), *Soviet Legal Philosophy*. Cambridge, Mass.: Harvard University Press, 1951.

Barnett, A. Doak, *A Perspective on Communist China*. New York: Praeger, 1962.

----------------, *Cadres, Bureaucracy and Political Power in Communist China*. New York: Columbia University Press, 1967.

Basic Problems in the Civil Law of the People's Republic of China. Peking: The Central Political-Judicial Cadres' School, 1958. Translated in English by U.S. Joint Publications Research Service, 1961.

Berman, Harold L., *Justice in the U.S.S.R.: An Interpretation of Soviet Law*. Cambridge, Mass.: Harvard University Press, 1963.

Blaustein, Albert P. (ed.), *Fundamental Legal Documents of Communist China*. South Hackensack, New Jersey: Fred B. Rothman & Co., 1962.

Boulais, Gui, *Manuel de code chinois*. Shanghai: Commercial Press, 1924.

Brandt, C., Schwarts, B., and Fairbank, J. K., *A Documentary History of Chinese Communism*. Cambridge, Mass.: Harvard University Press, 1952.

Chou, En-lai, *Report on the Work of the Government*. Peking: Foreign Language Press, 1954.

Chou, Fang, *Wo-kuo kuo-chia chi-kou* (The State Structure of Our Country). 2d ed. Peking: People's Press, 1957.

Chu, T'ung-tsu, *Chung-kuo fa-lu chih ju-chia-hua* Confucianization of Chinese Law). Peking: National Peking University Press, 1948.

--------------, *Law and Society in Traditional China*. Paris and The Hague: Mouton & Co., 1961.

-------------, *Local Government in China under the Ch'ing*. Cambridge, Mass.: Harvard University Press, 1962.

Cicero, *De Legibus*. English translation by Clinton Walker Keyes. Cambridge, Mass.: Harvard University Press, 1962.

Clubb, O. Edmund, *Twentieth Century China*. New York: Columbia University Press, 1964.

Cohen, Arthur A., *The Communism of Mao Tse-tung*. Chicago: The University of Chicago Press, 1964.

Communist China 1955-1959, Published by Center for International Affairs, East Asian Research Institute, Harvard University. Cambridge, Mass.: Harvard University Press, 1962.

de Bary, Wm. Theodore (ed.), *Sources of Chinese Tradition*. New York: Columbia University Press, 1960.

Dubs, H. H. (trans.), *The Works of Hsuntze*. London: A Probsthain, 1928.

Duez, Paul, and Debeyre, Guy, *Traite de droit administratif*. Paris: Dalloz, 1952.

Duyvendak, J. J. L. (trans.), *The Book of Lord Shang, A Classic of the Chinese School of Law*. London: The University of Chicago Press, 1928.

Engels, Friedrich, *The Origin of Family, Private Property, and the State*. London: Lawrence Wishart, 1941.

Escarra, Jean, *Le droit chinois*. Peking: Henri Vetch, 1936. English translation by G. R. Browne. Xerox reprint by Harvard Law School, 1961.

Fung, Yu-lan, *A History of Chinese Philosophy*. Peking: 1937. English translation by D. Bodde. Princeton, N.J.: Princeton University Press, 1953 (Vol. I); Leiden, 1953 (Vol. II).

Greene, Felix, *Awakened China*. Garden City, N.Y.: Doubleday, 1961.

Gudoshinikov, L. M., *Sudebyne Organy Kitaiskoi Narodnoi Respubliki* (Legal Organs of the People's Republic of China). English translation by JPRS, 1959.

Hazard, John N., *Settling Disputes in Soviet Society*. New York: Columbia University Press, 1960.

----------, *The Soviet System of Government.* 3rd ed. Chicago: The University of Chicago Press, 1964.

Hazard, John N. and Shapiro, Isaac, *The Soviet Legal System.* Dobbes Ferry, N.Y.: Oceana, 1962.

Ho, Han-chih, *Modern Revolutionary History of China.* Hong King: Sanlien, 1958.

Houn, Franklin W., *To Change a Nation: Propaganda and Indoctrination in Communist China.* Glencoe: Free Press, 1961.

------------, *Chinese Political Traditions.* Washington: Public Affairs Press, 1965.

Hsiao, King-chuan, *Rural China: Imperial Control in the Nineteenth Century.* Seattle: University of Washington Press, 1960.

Hulsewe, A. F. P., *Remnants of Han Law, Introductory Studies and an Annotated Translation of Chapters 22 and 23 of the History of the Former Han Dynasty.* Leiden: E. J. Brill, 1955.

Jan, George P. (ed.), *Government of Communist China.* San Francisco: Chandler, 1966.

Jones, Walter, *The Law and Legal Theory of the Greeks.* Oxford: Clarendon Press, 1956.

Kelsen, Hans, *The Communist Theory of Law.* New York: Praeger, 1955.

Kuo, Shou-hua, *The Public Security Organization and People's Police System of the Communist China.* Taipei: China Culture, 1957.

LaFave, Wayne R. (ed.), *Law in the Soviet Society*. Champaign, Ill.: University of Illinois Press, 1964.

Legge, James. (trans.), *The Texts of Confucianism*. Oxford: Clarendon, 1885.

----------, *The Chinese Classics*. Hong Kong: Hong Kong University Press, 1960.

Lenin, V. I., *Selected Works*. New York: International Publishers, 1937.

Levenson, Joseph R., *Confucian China and Its Modern Fate*. Berkeley and Los Angeles: University of California Press, 1958 and 1964 (2 Vols.).

Li, Ta, *Chung-hua jen-min king-ho-kuo hsien-fa chiang-hua* (Remarks on the Constitution of the Chinese People's Republic). Peking: People's Press, 1956.

Liao, W. K. (trans.), *The Complete Works of Han Fei Tze*. London, 1959.

Library of Congress, *Guide to Selected Legal Sources of Mainland China*. Washington, D. C., 1967.

Lin, Fu-shun (ed.), *Chinese Law — Past and Present: A Bibliography and Comment*. New York: East Asian Institute, Columbia University, 1966.

Mao, Tse-tung, *Selected Works of Mao Tse-tung*. 5 Vols. New York: International Publishers, 1954-1962.

----------, *On the Correct Handling the Internal Contradictions Among the People*. Peking: People's Press, 1957.

--------, *New Democratic Constitutionalism*. Peking: Foreign Language Press, 1960.

Maverich, Lewis, *et al, The Kuan-tzu*. Carbondale, Ill.: 1954.

Needham, Joseph, *Science and Civilization in China*. New York: Cambridge University Press, 1962.

Portisch, Hugo, *Red China Today*. Chicago: Quadrangle, 1966.

Principles of Criminal Law in the People's Republic of China. Edited by The Central Political-Judicial Cadres' School, 1958. Translated in English by the U.S. Joint Publications Research Service, 1962.

Principles of Marxism and Leninism. Peking: People's Press, 1959.

Pritchard, James B. (ed.), *Ancient Near Eastern Texts*. Princeton, N.J.: Princeton University Press, 1950.

Robson, William A., *Civilization and the Growth of Law*. New York: Macmillan, 1935.

Ryazanoff, D. (ed.), *The Communist Manifesto of Karl Marx and Friedrich Engels*. New York: Rusell & Rusell, 1963.

Schlesinger, Rudolf, *Soviet Legal Theory*. New York: Oxford University Press, 1945.

Schurmann, Frans, *Ideology and Organization in Communist China*. Berkeley and Los Angeles: University of California Press, 1966.

Som, Tjan Tjoe (trans.), *Po Hu T'ung, The Comprehensive Discussion in the White Tiger Hall.* 2 Vols. Leiden: E. J. Brill, 1949-1952.

Staunton, George Thomas, *Ta Tsing Leu Lee, Being the Fundamental Laws, and a Selection from the Supplementary Statutes of the Penal Code of China.* London: T. Cadell & W. Davies, 1810.

Tang, Peter S. H., *Communist China Today.* 2d ed. Washington: Research Institute on the Sino-Soviet Bloc, 1961.

Tsao, Wen-yen, *The Law in China as Seen by Roscoe Pound.* Taipei: China Culture, 1953.

van der Sprankel, Sybille, *Legal Institutions in Modern China.* London: The Athlone Press, 1962.

Vyshinsky, A. Y., *The Law of the Soviet State.* English translation by Hugh W. Babb. New York: Macmillan, 1948.

Wei, Henry, *Courts and Police in Communist China.* Montgomery, Alabama: Resources Institute, Air University, 1955.

Yang, Ch'ing-k'un, *The Chinese Family in the Communist Revolution.* Cambridge, Mass.: MIT Press, 1959.

Yang, Y. C., *Chung-kuo chin-dai fa-chih shih* (A History of Modern Chinese Legal System). Taipei: China Culture, 1958.

Articles and Periodicals

Bodde, D., "Myths of Ancient China," in *Mythologies of the Ancient World,* ed. by Samuel N. Kramer. New York: Doubleday Anchor Books, 1961.

218

--------, "Basic Concepts of Chinese Law: The Genesis and Evolution of Legal Thought in Traditional China," *Proceedings of the American Philosophical Society*, Vol. 107 (1963).

Bonnichon, Andre, "Law in Communist China," *International Commission of Jurists*, 1955.

Bulletin of the International Commission of Jurists, No. 8 (December 1958).

Chang Chiang Jih Pao (Chang-chiang Daily, Hankow), 1952. 1954.

Chang, Chien, "Our Country's System of Education and Rehabilitation Through Labor," *Political-Legal Research*, No. 6 (1959).

Chang, Chih-jang, "The Mission of Our Courts and the Experience of the Soviet Courts," *Political-Legal Research*, No. 1. (1954).

--------, "The People's Democratic Legal System of Our Country," *Political-Legal Research*, No. 6 (1956).

Chang, Hao, "The Position and Function of Socialist Laws in People's Democratic Dictatorship," *Political-Legal Research*, No. 4 (1962).

Chang, Mou, "Thorough Separation from the Bourgeois Concept of Law," *Political-Legal Research*, No. 6 (1958).

Chang, Pu, "Destroying Thoroughly the Old Legal System and Liquidating Bourgeois Legal Thinking," *Political-Legal Research*, No. 2 (1964).

Chang, T. C., "Policy Is the Soul of Law," *Political-Legal Research*, No. 3 (1958).

Chang, Tzu-pei, "Censure the Bourgeois Principle of the Judge's Free Evaluation of Evidence," *Political-Legal Research*, No. 2 (1958).

Chao, Ch'ing, "Several Problems Concerning Law and Policy," *Science of Law*, No. 2 (1958).

Chao, Pin-lin, *et al*, "The Lawyer System and Criminal Procedure in Our Country," *Chiao-hsueh yu yen-chiu* (Teaching and Research, Peking), No. 23 (1955).

Chao, W. C., "How Do the People's Procuratorates Do Their Investigation and Prosecution Work," *Science of Law*, No. 8 (1957).

Ch'en, Li-ping, "The Judicial Organs Must Resolutely Obey the Leadership of the Party," *Chun-chung (The Masses, Peking)*, No. 8 (December 1958).

Ch'eng, Chi-yung, "Following the Leadership of the Chinese Communist Party Is the Basic Principle of the Organizations and Activities of the State Organs," *Science of Law*, No. 6 (1957).

Cheng, Jung-ping, "Lawyers Must Serve the Socialist Legal System," *Science of Law*, No. 2 (1958).

Chien, Chia-chu, "The Social and Economic System During the Transitional Period of Our Country," *Political-Legal Research*, No. 3 (1955).

Chiu, Szu, "Chinese Socialist Law," *Political-Legal Research* No. 4 (1962).

Chiu, Vermier Y., "Marriage Laws of the Ch'ing Dynasty, the Republic of China and Communist China," *Comtemporary China*. Vol. II (1956-1957).

Chou, Heng-yuan, "On the Right to Defense of the Accused in the CRiminal Procedure of Our Country," *Political-Legal Research,* No. 3 (1956).

Chou, Hsin-min, "The Nature and Tasks of the People's Procuratorates," *Political-Legal Research,* No. 4 (1954).

----------, "Law Is a Sharp Weapon of Class Struggle," *People's Daily,* October 28, 1964.

Chou, Shih-chieh, "A Preliminary Study of Legal Relationship in Civil Procedure," *Chiao-hsueh Chien-pao* (Teaching Bulletin), No. 26 (June 1957).

Cohen, Jerome A., "The CRiminal Process in the People's Republic of China: An Introduction," *Harvard Law Review,* January 1966.

---------, "Chinese Mediation on the Eve of Modernization," *California Law Review,* August 1966.

Dai, S. Y., "Government and Law in Communist China," *Current History,* September 1961.

Fang, Yen, "Making the Marriage Law Work," *China Reconstructs,* No. 5 (1953).

Fu, S. L., "The New Marriage Law of People's Republic of China," *Contemporary China,* Vol. I (1955).

Fu, Weng, "Talk on the History of Adjudication of Cases," *Kuang Ming Daily,* March 20, 1962.

Ginsburgs, G., "Soviet Sources on the Law of the Chinese People's Republic," *Toronto Law Journal,* Vol. 18 (1968).

Gurr, Re-bing, "How I Learned to be A Judge," *Political-Legal Research*, No. 3 (1965).

Hazard, John N., "Soviet Socialism and the Conflict of Law," *Military Law Review*, January 1963.

--------, "Unity and Diversity in Socialist Law," *Law and Contemporary Problem*, Vol. 30 (1965).

Ho, Ssu-ching, "Marxist Theory of State and Law - in Commemoration of the 136th Birthday of Marx," *Political-Legal Research*, No. 1 (1954).

Hong Kong Times (Hong Kong), February, 1956.

Houn, Franklin W., "Communist China's New Constitution," *The Western Political Quarterly*, June 1955.

Hsia, Tao-tai, "Communist China's First Decade: Justice and the Law," *The New Leader*, June 22, 1959.

Hsiao, Yung-ching, "A Preliminary Approach to the Study of the History of the Chinese Legal System," *Political-Legal Research*, No. 3 (1965).

Hsin-hua yueh-pao (New China Monthly): later, *Hsin-hua pan yueh-kan* (New China Biweekly), 1956.

Hucker, Charles O., "The Traditional Chinese Censorate and the New Peking Regime," *American Political Science Review*, Vol. 45 (1951).

Jen Min Jih Pao, (People's Daily, Peking), 1950-1966.

Jo, Chuan. "The Party's Control of the Judiciary in China," *Soviet Survey*, April/June 1958.

Kao, Ko-lin, "Work of the Supreme People's Court Since 1955," *Current Background*, May 4, 1959.

Keng, I-tai, "Protecting the Party's Leadership in the People's Courts; Refuting the Absurd Contention of Trial Independence," *Cheng-fa chiao-hsueh* (Political-Legal Teaching), No. 1 (1958).

Kuang Ming Jih Pao (Kuang Ming Daily), 1952-1966.

Kwang Chow Jih Pao (Canton Daily), 1957.

Lee, Luke T., "Chinese Communist Law: Its Background and Development," *Michigan Law Review*, Vol. 60 (1962).

Leng, Shao-chuan, "The Lawyer in Communist China," *International Commission of Jurists*, Summer 1962.

--------, "Post Constitutional Development of People's Justice in China," *International Commission of Jurists*, Vol. 103 (1965).

Ling, Piao, "Chinese Communist Policies and Laws on the Cities," *Tsukuo* (Fatherland), September 1964.

Liu, K'un-lin, "On Independence of Courts, Subject Only to Law," *Political-Legal Research*, No. 1 (1955).

Liu, Tzu-chiang, "Thorough Criticism of Bourgeois Thinking in the Work of the People's Lawyers," *Science of Law*, No. 2 (1958).

Lubman, Stanley, "Mao and Mediation: Politics and Dispute Resolution in Communist China," *California Law Review*, Vol. 55, November 1967.

‒‒‒‒‒‒‒, "Forms and Functions in the Chinese Criminal Process," *Columbia Law Review*, April 1969.

McAleavy, Henry, "The People's Courts in Communist China," *The American Journal of Comparative Law*, Vol. 11, 1962.

Michael, Franz, "The Role of Law in Traditional, Nationalist and Communist China," *The China Quarterly*, Vol. 9 (January-March 1962).

Mitsunari, Kawaski, "The Attorney System," *Chugoku No Ho To Shakai* (Chinese Law and Society), Japan, 1960.

The New York Times, 1957, 1964.

The Orient (Hong Kong), January 1964.

Political-Legal Research (Peking), "Soviet Courts and Procuracy", No. 4 (1954).

Pound, Roscoe, "Comparative Law and History as Bases for Chinese Law," *Harvard Law Review*, May 1948.

Sarkar, S. C., "Judiciary in China," *India Quarterly*, October-December 1957.

Schwartz, Benjamin, "On Attitude Toward Law in China," in *Government under Law and the Individual*, edited and published by the American Council of Learned Societies, January 25, 1957.

Shih, Liang, "The Judicial System in New China," *People's China*, No. 12 (June 16, 1957).

Steiner, Arthur H., "Ideology and Politics in Communist China," *The Annals of the American Academy of Political and Social Sciences*, January 1959.

Tao, Lung-sheng, "The Criminal Law of Communist China," *Cornell Law Quarterly*, Vol. 52 (Fall 1966).

Tay, A. E., "Law in Communist China," *Sydney Law Review*, October 1969.

Tung, Pi-wu, "Judicial Work in China in the Past Year," *Current Background*, July 3, 1956.

-------, "The Legal System of China," *Current Background*, October 16, 1956.

Wang, Ju-chi, "The Functions and Organization of Soviet Attorneys," *Political-Legal Research*, No. 6 (1955).

Wang, Kan-yu, "Some Insights Gained From the Establishment of the New Lawyer System," *Political-Legal Research*, No. 2 (1956).

Wang, Ming, "How the People's Court of P'eng Lai Ch'u, Shanghai Municipality, Learned (A Campaign of) Speeches on Law," *Science of Law*, No. 8 (1958).

--------, "The Major Significance of the People's Adjustment Work in Resolving Contradictions Among the People," *Political-Legal Research*, No. 2 (1960).

Wang, Ya-tung, "Judicial Work Must Resolutely Carry Out the Mass Line," *Science of Law*, No. 9 (1958).

Woodsworth, K. C., "The Legal System of the People's Republic of China," *Canadian Bar Journal*, Vol. 4 (1961).

--------, "Family Law and Resolution of Domestic Disputes in The People's Republic of China," *McGill Law Journal*, Vol. 169 (1967).

Wu, Ta-yin, "The Nature and Characteristics of the Socialist Law," *Science of Law*, No. 3 (1958).

Wu, Te-feng, "To Defend the Socialist Legal System," *Political-Legal Research*, No. 1 (1958).

Wu, Yu-su, "Censure the Bourgeois Principle of Presumption of Innocence," *Political-Legal Research*, No. 2 (1958).

Yang, Kuang-teh, "Going to Law in Peking," *China Reconstructs*, No. 5 (1956).

Yang, Tzu-wei, "Report of the Work of Tsinghai Provincial Higher Court," *Tsinghai Daily*, December 15, 1959.

Yee, Franks S. H., "Chinese Communist Police and Courts," *Journal of Criminal Law*, May/June 1957.

Yeh, Ku-lin, "Thoroughly Developing the Construction of Socialistic Service Is a Function of People's Mediation Work," *Political-Legal Research*, No. 4 (1964).

Reports

Cheng-fa yen-chiu (Political-Legal Research). *Report on Chinese Law*. A Report Prepared by the Editor, 1962.

En-lai Chou, *Political Report to the 8th National Congress of the Communist Party of China*, 1956.

Liu, Shao-chi, *Report on the Draft Constitution of the People's Republic of China,* 1954.

People's Procurator-General. *Explanatory Report on the Office of People's Procurator-General,* 1952.

Tung, Pi-wu, *Report on the Work of the Supreme People's Court,* 1956.

Unpublished Material

Boiter, Albert, "Socialist Courts in the U.S.S.R." Unpublished Ph.D. Dissertation, Columbia University, 1965.

Index

Adversary system, 8

Analogy, 10, 57, 140, 145-146

Bar Associations, 188-189

Basic Courts, 171-172, 174

Capitalism, 2, 77, 82, 126
    abolition of, 69, 127
    industry and, 121-125
    philosophy of, 112

Censors, 182-183

Children, 39, 128-129

Ch'ing dynasty, 9, 10-11, 35-37, 40-41, 208

Chou En-lai, 170

Civil Law
Communist, 57, 63, 86, 104, 107, 117-140, 148,
168, 178, 181, 208
courts, 171, 172, 174
Nationalist, 41-42
pre-modern, 11

Class
division, 66, 68, 84-85, 115, 131-133
exploitation, 67, 70, 76, 78, 83, 111-112
nature of law, 117
ruling, 82, 118, 134, 143
working, 81, 85, 86, 112, 115, 132, 205

Communist Party
government and, 58, 60, 64, 113, 121, 141
leadership, 56, 76, 81, 85, 88
members, 57, 63, 168
policies of, 78-99, 107, 110-113, 127, 133, 143,
150, 169, 205, 207
techniques, 80, 113-114, 175

Conciliation Commission, 172-173

Confucian school, 8, 31, 34, 35, 37-39, 40, 183

Confucian values, 3, 7, 12, 26-29, 208

Constitution of the People's Republic, 57, 108, 109,
114, 122-124, 126-127, 141, 142, 171, 179, 180,
187

Contracts, 125-126, 136

Counties, 12, 135, 167, 168

Criminal Law
code, 104, 178
Communism and, 64, 141-150, 207

    courts, 61, 107, 171-172, 174
    diplomatic immunity, 136
    Nationalist period, 41-42, 130
    nature of, 57

Divorce, 10-11, 58, 173

Education, 2, 57, 91, 116, 143, 147-148, 150, 173, 177

Engels, Friedrich, 68, 75

Extra-legal bodies, 12-13, 149, 168, 207, 208

Fa, 13, 14-16, 27, 29, 34-35, 79, 84, 183

Feudalism, 8, 27, 35, 46, 80, 82, 121, 128

Guilt, assumption of, 34, 57, 181

Habeas Corpus, 41

Han dynasty, 9, 15, 35, 39

Higher Courts, 174

Hsiao Ho, 9

Hsing, 13, 15-16, 84

Huand Ti, 8

Intermediate Courts, 173-174

Judges
    educational role, 2
    old laws and, 12, 38
    People's Republic, 57, 62, 67, 86, 108, 110,
        112-114, 148, 169-171, 174, 176, 178, 181,
        185, 186
    Soviet, 61, 79, 189

Judicial Committees, 174-175

Khrushchev, Nikita, 62

Kuomintang, *see* Nationalist Government

Labor, 18, 57-58, 60, 71, 76, 108, 148-150, 168, 177

Law Codification Committee, 89-90, 104

Lawyers, 12, 61-63, 112, 168, 181, 183-192

Legalist school, 8-9, 15, 26-27, 30-34, 35, 37, 39,
    183

Lenin, Nikolain, 50, 55, 59, 68-72, 74-75, 78-79, 81,
    83-85, 87, 88, 91, 108, 150, 170-171, 179

Li, 2-3, 16, 18, 27-30, 33, 34, 40, 79, 129-131, 183,
    206, 209

Li K'uei, 8

Mao Tse-tung, 5, 55, 63-64, 79, 86, 87-89, 91, 107-
    108, 128, 150, 170, 177

Marriage, 39, 40, 56, 58, 108, 128-130, 135, 139, 173

Marx, Karl, 5, 50, 55, 59, 65, 67-70, 72, 74-75, 78-
    79, 81, 84-85, 87-89, 132, 167, 170-171

Mass trials, 60

Mediation, 3, 57, 63, 208

Ming dynasty, 9, 35-37

Nationalist government, 9, 30, 40-43, 55-68, 89, 103,
143, 169-170, 183-184, 186

National People's Congress, 63, 109, 137, 138-139,
140, 142, 184, 175, 177

Organic Law of the People's Courts, 174-175, 177-178,
187

Police, 60-62, 81, 168, 208

Political crime, 57, 87, 103

Privileged groups, 35-37

Procedural rule, 58

Procuratorate, 58, 61-62, 139, 175, 179-183, 204-205

Propaganda, 57

Property, 39, 67, 119, 121, 123-125, 127

Punishment, 10-11, 27, 30, 32, 34, 37-38, 57-58, 60,
83-84, 91, 143, 145-150, 167, 168, 173

Reform, to, 55, 62-64, 91, 147-148

Religion, 14-16-19

Reprimand, 148, 150

Retroactivity, 143-145

Rule of Law, 115, 203-204, 206

Shih Liang, 88, 89, 173

Social groups, 7, 74-75

Social hierarchy, 10, 26, 28, 30, 35, 37, 39, 56, 140

Special courts, 175-178

Stalin, 5, 61-62, 64, 72, 73

Sui dynasty, 9

Sung dynasty, 36

Sun Yat-Sen, 41, 183

Supreme People's Court, 88-89, 104, 111, 120, 137, 139, 142, 167, 169, 171, 175, 177, 180

Surveillance, 148-149

Tang dynasty, 9, 36

Teng Hsiao-p'ing, 168

Torture, 34, 36, 40

Tsin dynasty, 8

Union of Soviet Socialist Republics, 4, 5, 59-65, 68-69, 71.